The *Missouri* *Review*

Volume XIX Number 1   1996

University of Missouri-Columbia

EDITOR	MANAGING EDITOR
Speer Morgan	Greg Michalson

ASSOCIATE EDITORS

William Peden, Jo Sapp, Evelyn Somers

OFFICE MANAGER

Dedra Earl

SENIOR ADVISORS

Mary Creger, Reeves Hamilton, Kristen Harmon,
Hoa Ngo, Kirstin Rogers, Kris Somerville, Jeff Thomson

ADVISORS

Tracy Benbrook, Seth Bro, Ed Fogarty,
Joel Huggins, Stephanie Komen, Julie Laune,
Sarah Oster, David Schlansker, Melissa Wright

INTERNS

Brian Baker, Rebecca Fuhrman, Brad Hauck,
Tuan Heidenreich, Amy Kennebec,
Able Klainbaum, Elizabeth Knapp, Nick Mullendore

The Missouri Review is published by the College of Arts & Science of the University of Missouri-Columbia, with private contributions and assistance from the Missouri Arts Council and the National Endowment for the Arts.

Web Page Site at http://www.missouri.edu/~moreview

Cartoons in this issue by Charles Barsotti.

The editors invite submissions of poetry, fiction, and essays of a general literary interest with a distinctly contemporary orientation. Manuscripts will not be returned unless accompanied by a stamped, self-addressed envelope. Please address all correspondence to The Editors, *The Missouri Review*, 1507 Hillcrest Hall, University of Missouri, Columbia, Missouri 65211.

SUBSCRIPTIONS

1 year (3 issues), $19.00
2 years (6 issues), $35.00
3 years (9 issues), $45.00

Copyright © 1996 by The Curators of the University of Missouri
ISSN 0191 1961   **ISBN** 1-879758-16-4
Typesetting by HiTec Typeset   Printed by Thomson-Shore
Distributed by: Ingram Periodicals and B. DeBoer

The *Missouri* Review

CONTENTS   1996

POETRY (cont)

ESSAY

BOOK REVIEWS

"AS BUSY AS HE IS, BILL GATES HAS A NEW BOOK OUT."

Foreword

One of the legends about the life of thirties blues musician Robert Johnson is that one afternoon at a lonely Mississippi crossroads he made a deal with the devil, trading his soul for genius. Some years ago, I heard an otherwise intelligent writer (of some note) claim in a public reading that this event had actually occurred. It always surprises me when people flatly state metaphoric ideas to be "so true" as to be the same as literal truth. I questioned him about it and he eventually peevishly admitted that he didn't *really* believe that there was a devil who went around appearing and offering deals. Yet having admitted this, he reaffirmed that Robert Johnson had made such a deal with the devil anyway. More or less.

On such non sequiturs conversations die.

Yet he was right about the legend being compelling. The mysterious Johnson appears to have flowered quickly from a so-so harmonica player in 1929 to a full-blown guitar and songwriting genius in the mid-thirties. The "crossroads" of the story is part of its appeal, too, because it suggests one of those moments when one has a clear but dangerous choice. In legends and myths we construct worlds with such big choices. The devil makes his offer, you decide.

Of course, real life isn't usually that clear cut. We sometimes don't recognize turns in the road. For any number of reasons—busyness, preoccupation, the disinclination to think about certain things—we may choose either without knowing or without attending to what we know. We flow along like water taking what seems to be, but seldom is, the path of least resistance.

One of the preoccupations of literature, particularly storytelling, is to reconstruct the connection between character and fate. Literature is in this sense a religious enterprise: it asserts, as an article of faith, that there is a conjunction between who we are, what we choose to do, and what happens to us. The weave between character, choice, and outcome can sometimes be perplexing and subtle, but there is finally a pattern.

In this issue's prose, the stakes are high. Characters come to crossroads almost as dramatic as in the legend of Robert Johnson and the devil. In Deborah Way's Editors' Prize-winning story "You Think I Care," a teenage girl, who thinks she is invulnerable, runs smack against the fact that she isn't. The story depicts the phenomenal mental agility with which the teenager tries to hold onto her self-image no matter what. In Lloyd Zimpel's amazing historically set story "Beiderman and the Hard Words," the fates mistake the patriarch of a pioneering family for Indiana Jones and keep imposing challenges, almost comical in their extremity, on him and his family, testing them beyond all reasonable limits. Lauren Slater's personal essay "Black Swans" describes equally bizarre calamities of a psychological sort as Slater relates her own experience with an obsessive-compulsive disorder.

Adults in love can be almost as helpless and vulnerable as kids, as is the case for Nancy Kincaid's smitten middle-aged professor in "Why Richard Can't." Kincaid seems to wonderfully empathize with her male protagonist as he wrestles with the question of whether he should stick with the unfulfilling known or take a leap into the promising unknown. Paula Huston's "Serenissima" depicts a similarly powerful attraction, a woman's love for a place that represents freedom and romance to her but where she encounters something so unexpected and incongruous that it haunts her for life.

Jon Billman's story "When We Were Wolves" and Scott Boylston's "Captains By Default" concern boys' games and how they can get out of control. Both are about that thin line between playing by the rules and terrible destruction, how often we may skate up to the line, flirt with it, almost cross it—or indeed may do so and change our lives forever.

Kathy Fagan's Editors' Prize-winning poems are very much crossroads poems that explore emotional thresholds and imagine paths not taken. Our other poets—Liz Rosenberg, Kevin Stein and Julia Wendell—all write about the influences of obsessive family relationships, failed or successful or stricken, that can dominate fate and personality, pushing one's sense of self and security to the edge.

Donald Morrill's essay, "The One Strong Flower I Am," another Editors' Prize winner, acquaints us with the nebulous, confusing job of working with "at risk" children, many of whom come from worlds that are already over the line. They live surrounded by choices between bad and awful, but Morrill is intrigued less by their edginess and confusion than by their relative decency and their capability, even in the midst of chaos, for creativity.

William Maxwell's interview by Kay Bonetti is one of the most entertaining we've seen in some time. It tells of a long life of writing and editing. Maxwell is a short-story writer and novelist of the first order, who went to work at *The New Yorker* in 1936 at a salary of $35 a week and over the next four decades became an important behind-the-scenes editorial influence on American fiction.

Hearty congratulations to this year's Editors' Prize winners, Deborah Way, Donald Morrill and Kathy Fagan. And special congratulations to last year's fiction winner, Deborah Galyan, whose prize story, "The Incredible Appearing Man" has just been selected for the upcoming edition of *Best American Short Stories*.

SM

" HE'S PANICKING, INSPECTOR. HE'S OBVIOUSLY
LOST HIS STRUNK AND WHITE."

"A POET?! NOW LISTEN TO YOUR MOTHER, DEAR, THROW HIM BACK AND GO GET A DOCTOR OR LAWYER."

BEIDERMANN AND THE HARD WORDS
/ Lloyd Zimpel

1876

A UG. 2. AN OVER-HEATED wind all day, and the dust that rides on it—not simple dust but dirt itself, the earth itself. The rags Ma stuffs in door and window sills hold back only some; and grit in her kitchen, on the oilcloth, pots, in the water-pail, a skin of it everywhere, near gives her fits. With grit in our teeth, we spit black.

That wind is too much to work in for more than a few hours, in that the horses will stand tail to it, heads lowered and eyes hooded, tails blowing back across their rears. Among us it goes unsaid, though bursting to be said, there will be little crop anywhere this season in this part of Dakota; except in the small greener bottoms of the river where, for all that the heat goes as it does everywhere, yet the baking wind is less. Those fields are the lucky Beidermann's, indeed, the blessed Beidermann's, for it is as if the drouth chooses to pass him by; his good fortune being that the greater of his land lies where the river still shows something more than a damp stain; at which our cattle contend with his along its snaking length, a hundred heads tossing and tails whipping against the flies that cover them like a coat of blacking wherever mud is not crusted, as it is on their legs and underbellies, baked there like armor-plating. Today, the twins peel off sheets of it from a skinny heifer before she summons strength enough to stagger free....

Aug. 3. God gives no quarter, sending nary a cloud, nor one the size of a baby's hand, against the fearsome sun, which murders any beneath it that turn for a moment careless. Henry, coming home from the North section with the hides off two calves gone under from this onslaught, rides in himself dizzied and half-addled; and here it is well into the still-hot night and he has watered himself thoroughly, inside and out, and only now does he come into my lamp's light, and sighing heavily takes a little of the meat and potato Ma left out for him....

Aug. 4. Even as he stands and watches, vows Otto, he can discern the decline of the water in our well. It is nearly so; against the fading wetness of the stone wall it descends the width of a girl's finger each day; and the rope paid out today to fetch a bucketful exceeds by my arm's length the amount required to do the job after the spring thaw. Much of what we take from it goes to keep Ma's garden decent; and she begrudges more of it than I would to her damned geraniums, which flout their health while the grass six feet from them is dead, and the leaves on the box-elder by the porch are gray, not green.....

The twins return late from a day helping Beidermann scrape up a dam at a trickle of a spring he has lately, most providentially, discovered, and they report the pool sufficient to provide the stock consigned thereabouts; even as Beidermann's home-place well, which they assisted in digging when he first came here, is no less full than when they dug it, say they. They express puzzlement then, why our own should drop, as if there is some flaw in my placement of it, done before they or any of the boys, excepting Otto, were even born; but my explanation that our bachelor neighbor draws from a different reserve, appears to fade away unheard. There is this too, left unsaid, for it would seem sour: that Beidermann's good fortune does not waver much, however the destinies of others are jarred and twisted as God sees fit to do so often; and if such blessings result from our staunch neighbor's close attention to his land and animals, why, then those of us who labor no less strenuously, have cause to ponder how even-handedly the destinies of men on Earth are administered from on High, and to ask in a whisper behind closed doors, whether some are not being dealt a shorter hand than others.....

Aug. 8. Beidermann arrives today for the loan of our rake, as if to impress upon us that he has hay to use it on while we do not. His massive team is in empty harness, himself astride the mare, and swinging off that broad back he says: I come along the bluff to the South, and I see your stock there are mostly skin and bones. God-damn this heat!

You have that wrong, says I. God is not likely to damn it, as it is Him who sends it.

From under the brim of his cloth hat, Beidermann's cool squint rests upon me. Another time he might laugh. The two of us have had our words before on Providence and the workings of

Nature, and Mister Beidermann makes it clear that he sets no store in help nor hindrance by way of Heaven.

So you have the right to think, says our philosopher neighbor, but I will tell you this: it is just a turn of the big wheel we are up against, and when it turns more we will get better times. There are rewards due us all.

Yes, say I. Rewards in the Hereafter. And I ask you, sir, who is it that spins that big wheel of yours?

As always, Beidermann has his answer ready: From the looks of your animals, I would say it is the Devil, eh, boys? He nods to the twins with a wink, and the two of them look to me, reluctant to say: Beidermann is right, look at how he prospers. I know they have long been persuaded by the able Beidermann and his ways; in this easy trust being the very opposite of my older boys, who stand warily aside and watch.

Beidermann backs his team over the rake's tongue and says: If I get two-thirds of what I made last year, I will count myself a lucky man.

Count yourself that, then, says I, for I have not put up nearly half a crop, and there is nothing for another cutting.

Beidermann grunts, a half-angry sound that means no commiseration with my lot, but is instead a noise of displeasure at his unturning wheel, that it is stuck in this rut. . . .

Aug. 10.

> *We dropped the seed o'er hill and plain*
> *Beneath the sun of May. . . .*

It is now the sun of August and another story, for the wheat we have seen so far is all we shall see: a stunted lot, indeed, not half-grown, kernels small as lice and hard as stone, and we will cut it for straw for want of another choice; Otto sensibly declaring it is a few weeks' winter fodder not otherwise come by and which we will badly need. There is abundant time to carry out the bleak reaping chore, for we are freed from all labor of a normal harvest in this sun-struck country. Among us all, only Beidermann needs extra hands to put up his so-called two-thirds. Cornelius and the twins will take a team and rack over; and doubtless he also has the exchange of help from Krupp and all the others as well. . . .

Aug. 11. Ma looks over my shoulder just now, having read her night's piece, this from the book of Jeremiah, that I must hear. He tells us, says Ma, that we are brought

> *to a plentiful country to eat the fruit thereof,*
> *but now we have forsaken the fountain of living*
> *waters, and hewed out cisterns, broken cisterns, that*
> *can hold no water; and then, we hast polluted the land*
> *with our whoredoms and wickedness. Therefore the showers*
> *have been witholden and there hath been no latter rain....*

Well, Ma, says I, that is Jeremiah and this is us. But it is something to chew on, all right. There is no question about the broken cisterns and no rain—but what is this whoredom and wickedness? Unless we have been missing something big, the only thing that comes close to that in this country is Beidermann and the Widow Jenssen.

Oh, shhh, says Ma, piqued. It is not them. It is the sinfulness of us all.

That may be so, says I, and Beidermann is sure one of the sinners, but still his cistern did not break, did it?

Aug. 12. Henry reports that Krupp, whom he encounters on the West section setting out poison baits for a prairie wolf he thinks chewed up one of his calves, now favors us with rumors of grasshoppers south of Skiles, twenty miles therefrom. But that is Krupp; and these are rumors in a country where hope goes under often, so that a man learns to expect disaster. As a full moon is certain in its time, so is Emil Krupp known to adumbrate catastrophe: When matters are grim, they will grow worse before getting better; it will become hotter before it cools; drier before it rains; colder before it warms; a deeper freeze before thaw; hail before harvest, &c, &c,—the promise of calamity swiftly seen, so that one's guard may be raised against even harder times, and the heart prepare itself to bear the harder event, which is sure to occur....

But as for Krupp's grasshoppers we must wait and see, although without happy anticipation. I have seen them more than once, and it is another kind of world they bring. Fire is no worse, for flames can be fought and sometimes quelled.

But we shall see. It is thus every August—rumors of the dread plague. So has it been since Biblical times when it was the dread locust, which old Reinhardt calls them still—locusts; as if he can, in all his tottering years, remember them from that very time.

Aug. 14. What is it we are meant to do, then? The sun will soon take all. The hot wind punishes without a moment's surcease. We all grow uglier, nor do we give a thought to it that we do. Otto, the oldest, always steadfast, comes from the dinner table, turns on the porch step, and abruptly vows that he will leave this God-damned place, saying he should have done so long ago, it being an unfit place for white men; and here he has wasted a life of thirty-five years upon it. And for all that this is the land that I chose—while not my first choice, given the railroad's gluttony, but my choice still—Otto in his torment puts my judgment into question, although I feel no call to answer, for the boy has no malice in him; it is all despair.

But it is something other than despair in his next brother, Harris, who shows a constant agitation of discontent, barely contained, so that his own mother, with her heart open to all her seven sons equally, looks on him with doubts, as if he is visited upon us as a family test, with his cruel, black moods and sour way.

Now he mocks Otto, saying: Oh, yes, maybe you should pull out for the sand country where all the pickings are rich, eh? Cook yourself up a nice batch of burrs and nettles for your supper, eh?

Long past taking issue with his peevish brother, Otto says: Only a God-damned fool would try to hang on here year after year. And he adds bitterly: It looks like I am one of them.

But I know that among them all he is one who will not go, for as the poet knows,

> Not what we would, but what we must,
> Makes up the sum of living. . . .

Aug. 15. In the creek in our North pasture—but there is no creek: tiny, bitter pools, a trickle sometimes, the foul water insufficient for a man to wash his feet. This, reports Henry, as if he has come up with some jarring news, is the worst he has ever seen it.

For some, any new affliction is the worst. I have seen it worse.

Aug. 16. The twins report that the busy Beidermann has cut a good crop of hay off his most southern acreage, so good that he has traded a portion of it to Reinhardt for a hog, which the old man cannot feed, but Beidermann can.... Our Beidermann does his business as if conditions of the drouth impose no more hardship on him than would any sunny day, and therefore the rest of us, in our complaining, are spineless as chickens. Surely, this rubs the most easy-going among us the wrong way. For me, or Krupp, or Reinhardt, this Beidermann is little more than a visitor: hardly three seasons in this territory—whatever part of the World he has graced in his undisclosed past—so his high-horse manner cannot derive from special knowledge of what prevails here, among us, for he is innocent of that. How many others have I seen set themselves up in full confidence one year, and the next, when from sun or fire, hail or storm, for all that man and wife and every child works dawn to dusk, they get so far behind that they must crawl with their tails between their legs back to the wife's folks back East? I can hardly count their number.

And still our Beidermann does more than well, given these grim times, where the rest of us do not, as if such lordly assurance generates its own success, even at a time when failure is in the wind itself; and if that wind bears the rumored grasshoppers to us, it is more than failure and even the valiant Beidermann's certitude will shrink to the size of a grain of my wheat....

Aug. 17. Early, the day has some body to it, but with the rising of the sun, there is only the singular dimension of Old Sol. Heat, heat, and more of it; the air is thinned by it and even the wind lacks heft; so that two breaths are needed to do the work of one, and birds flying through seem weakly borne, though few birds fly: a single crow flaps high, another soon follows, both silent where usually they are the noisiest of creatures.

Aug. 18. So, it is no rumor but a prophecy—or possibly a grand prank, that grasshoppers come in a season where there is so little for them to destroy. But come they do, in dread abundance.... At noon, August hastens across the yard and calls through the screendoor in the porch where I am washing up for dinner: They are here!

Over his shoulder in the Western sky comes one small, dark cloud, their cruel vanguard, which as I watch twists somewhat to the North to reveal broadside the tail of itself; that small cloud being only the head of a long stream in the shape of a great tadpole, rising up from some hidden place, miles off, while its tail reaches to the horizon.

They are headed more North, I say.

No, says August. You are fooling yourself. They are coming to us, for certain.

His words are their invitation. That thickening cloud swerves again, enlarging itself somehow, once, twice. Ma, coming to the door quilts in hand, cries: Cover the garden! They will have it all! It is little enough, her garden, but the last healthy green left for us to look on.

With what? says August. Those quilts? What is it they will not eat?

My prayer is that they will still pass us up, at least in the main; but I hasten to the shed, August following, and the twins coming up on their ponies, from wherever they have been, and Otto and Cornelius coming from the barn; and from the shed we drag forth the cowhides stored there.

They will eat these, too, says Otto, flattening bean vines to lay the stiff hides across, but we cover what we can, while Ma spreads her quilts over her geraniums and the new strawberry plants....

The first of our visitors descend, no more than we might see on a normal summer's day. They gaily leap, not so much flying as gliding for great distance: another leap, another glide. But behind these few scouts the cloud unfolds, expands, becomes black as prairie smoke, as massive as the throngs of pigeons I have seen back East, spreads itself down on us; a crashing deluge, like buckets of hail crackling down. We have not finished tying cord around our sleeves and pants cuffs before they seethe over us, clinging for an instant and dropping away. The cowhides go thick with them, in overlapping layers, those on top covering those beneath, and another layer smothering those. Ma's quilts seem to change colors as the insects swarm across.

The twins, in awe and amazement, seeing this phenomenon for the first time with other than infant eyes, cease work and stand staring at the mounds crawling at their feet, and kick at them until Ma calls and they run, looking back at the sheet of insects settling at their heels, to the kitchen to help her renew her rag seals around windows and doors.

Around my legs the chickens flutter and hop with whimpering chirps, startled by the thin, dry buzz all around; and all the while peck away in a frenzy, scarcely moving from one spot, engorging themselves.

At the barn, Cornelius hollers for help to haul in the harness left draped on the fence, before it is eaten; the sweat-salted collars and breeching already clotted to double their size with the thronging insects. Cornelius scrapes them away in handfuls as he drags the harness to the safety of the barn; and they are thick as snow about my face as I go to help him: a crisp sting as one strikes skin, clinging until knocked away to make room for another; and a carpet of them underfoot—dozens crushed with the sound of crusted snow beneath each footfall.

From the barn door, above the windy sound of the besieging creatures, I hear the swine set up a contented snuffling as they suck up their rich supper in slobbering mouthfuls, hardly moving their long snouts to take up another pintful, so thickly do the insects clog their trough....

And still there come more, although there is no room for more. Miles away, in the West, a new wide sheen veers across the horizon, nearing us; the sun glints above on the membranes of their wings; a jewel-like sparkle all throughout their mass. The newcomers tumble in fist-sized lumps onto their brothers already here, locust upon locust, a half-dozen deep, now a dozen, as if they would eat through each other to get at the ground beneath that is already gnawed bare. By the chicken coop they come to the hens' thighs; some of the fowls already are so overstuffed they can barely move, and some foolish ones, filled to bursting, with beaks open gasp for air as they squat and tip to their sides; some are goners, and with time to butcher them now, before their feathers are chewed away and their meat polluted, they will be edible; but by tomorrow the tenderest portions of their flesh, having absorbed what they eat today, will taste vile.

I call to Otto: I have forgotten the horses. He waves a hand toward the upper pasture, where they stand nervously in a turning string, looking back with heads high; then their hind-ends swivel about and they look again.... Out in the pasture there are no birds. Where are the birds that rescued the Mormons? Every lark, every robin, is gone to hide....

Aug. 19. Midmorning, as the twins and Cornelius and Henry and I caulk the walls of the barn loft with dampened rags, that we might preserve such hay as we have rescued from the weather. I hear Henry mutter and I look up to see a wagon coming up our road through shallow drifts of grasshoppers; and if I did not recognize Beidermann, I would know his handsome team.

The Great Man cometh, says Henry in his wry way.

The twins run ahead, batting grasshoppers left and right from their faces. No less beleaguered, I come out of the barn as Beidermann pulls up his grand Percherons, which stand unsure against the invading insects, planting and unplanting each plate-sized hoof and killing grasshoppers each time; ears and eyes a-twitch, hides shivering.

Beidermann gives me a sprightly hallo. I will tell you something, he says. These sons-of-bitches will eat anything. Look here.

He lifts the mare's right front leg and runs the dirty fetlock through his fingers. Look! he says. They et it! Et the God-damned hair, they did. They will eat the hide right off your animals, you bet!

To my eye, the hair, dirty and ragged as it would naturally be, could have been chewed on or could not have been—there was no telling. But his horses stood like set-out meals here, and I sent the twins to fetch fly-bags for them, that they did not breathe in a suffocating dosage of grasshopper.

Thus far, Beidermann is happy to tell us, his own land has been spared—providentially so, says he—and tells us he watched from a mile's distance a plume like a flying serpent flow across the prairie and settle like smoke on his neighbors' fields, bypassing his own, toward which it at first seemed headed for certain. He does not ask what turned it, but makes his report as he busily twists a little bow into the cuff of each shirt sleeve, then tucks it tightly under itself to secure his sleeves against invasion. His pants he has already tied off with twine over the boot tops, his shirt's top button is fastened tight, so the reddish flesh of his neck puckers over the sweaty collar.

The Widow is under siege, too, Beidermann announces; a sizable tributary of the winged stream having descended upon her, allowing her clamorous geese to so stuff themselves, says Beidermann—the only one of us to summon a chuckle—that the gander has no honk left!...He has been at the Widow's the afternoon before—gallant though unadmitted suitor that he is—to battle the scourge with her while her two little girls, not the most sensible children in Creation, huddled in the house in terror, for they saw the voracious hordes as a sign the World was ending and they were doomed to die under a pile of clicking insects. Indeed, maybe not so silly—for who can foretell the final sign He will send up at the end...?

But Beidermann has more important information: it was while buying the Widow Jenssen's vegetables to remove them from the invader's predations, he tells us, that inspiration visited him. Now he points to its results: it is the awkward device he goes to unlimber from his wagon bed, brought along to me, he allows, that I may test its practical worth—and doubtless, stand impressed by Beidermann's genius.

He seems inordinately proud—for the straightforward Beidermann—of what he has fetched us. What it appears to be, as the twins rush to help him ease it off the wagon, is a large slab of sheet metal. It flops flat on the ground, sending grasshoppers spraying out from under it in all directions.

You see, lectures Beidermann, it will scoop them up, and into the coal oil you put back here, where they will die. Can we hitch one of your teams to it? He spits out his chaw, and is ready.

I am doubtful of his proposal, but in any event my animals are far afield, except the black gelding with which Harris plows a hasty, crooked furrow around the tomatoes, the upstruck earth I can see from the barn, more gray than black, so deep has the drouth penetrated; and into this shallow ditch Ma and August scoop what insects they can catch with their grain shovels—the insects leaping clear near as fast as they are shoveled in—and when there is a chance accumulation a few yards long, Harris lays over it a cover of straw which he sets afire, and joins his helpers in slapping at both errant flames and fleeing grasshoppers. Some few die. . . .

I point out my horses a half-mile off. I am not prone to fetch them for dubious purposes, so Beidermann unhesitatingly unfastens his mammoth animals from the wagon—they seem too grand for his trivial intention—and hooks them to the chains bolted to the far ends of his invention, which, it takes no careful inspection to see, might well be a section of the metal wall pulled from off the Skiles' saloon or livery barn: an eight- or ten-foot length, three-foot deep, which, Beidermann explains, will slide smooth and flat across the ground while being drawn by the chains he has just hooked up. In the back, a little trough having been hammered in and the back lip folded up, he now pours a gallon or two from the tin stored under his wagon seat, and this will drown the scooped-up insects. His preparations complete, Beidermann takes command of the contraption by two handles nailed to the far ends of the metal that bear in toward the center, where he walks, grasping the handles and changing direction by muscular force, as with a walking cultivator.

Captain Beidermann orders, and his animals, having stood to their limit against the irritating insects, surge into their collars, sending asail the gouts stuck to their wet cheekpieces, and Beidermann's invention cuts like a sharply swung blade into the uneven ground of my yard, slicing off hummocks and bulges as neatly as any road scraper as it bucks its way into the garden.

Beidermann does a lively dance to keep the thing in hand. We must admire his agility there—but that is all. This apparatus of his is no more than a piece of tin, a shiny trinket to distract a two-inch bug, and more suitable to a child and ponies than the looming Beidermann and his leviathan pair. . . .

As if their hero is achieving something here, the twins jump in delight, skipping behind, as Beidermann frantically hauls at reins and handles alike, one of each in each hand, and persuades his team past the cowhides with their crawling host, to the remnants of the potato vines, the last of their green stems no more than fibrous threads poking like nerve ends out of the boiling layer of grasshoppers, the potatoes themselves mostly out of reach underground, their stems too insubstantial for the gnawers to tunnel down through them as they do with the onions and radishes, to eat them from the inside out, leaving hollow balls in the earth. Onto this quivering carpet goes Beidermann, his horses hawing in a prance, jawing their bits like circus ponies, while the twins attend the rig's progress, having stationed themselves at either end—perhaps Beidermann has so instructed them—and leap to free the device when an edge catches, as it does, on a clod or hummock or digs cockeyed into the soft earth. Dust rises in a cloud around to obscure the mass of grasshoppers also rising—or it may be that it is the other way around and the grasshoppers do the obscuring: it is all a blur.

From under the eaves of the barn, Cornelius and Henry look on, and at the far end of the garden I see Harris pull up the gelding, and I know without seeing it, the scorn on his face. He drops the handles of the walking plow and with Ma and August turns to watch Beidermann's animated advance. The metal pan bounces high as if kicked from beneath, and whipsaws wildly as the leading edge catches here and there, flicking tongues of coal oil with each jerk until the twins are splattered head to toe as they wrestle the seesawing ends with shouts of half-delight and half-alarm.

Beidermann, the sweating helmsman, yells at his team, at the twins, at the grasshoppers, at God in His Heaven, perhaps; and I

wonder if he has lost command of more than just his contraption—
which is moving too fast: earth springing up before and flying
over behind. His horses cannot draw it slowly enough—no living
horses could—and his prey in its abundance leaps with ease from
out his path, and three feet over finds something else to chew.

Behind my shoulder, Otto says: Well, I see he got two hoppers
there, but looks like a million going the other way. . . .

Some few little beasts, to be sure, are sufficiently confounded
by Beidermann's device to jump into it. When he has made one
swath, Beidermann hauls up to wipe the sweat out his eyes;
he tips his machine sideways, and a few hundred oil-coated
grasshoppers slide into a bushel-sized greasy pile of dirt, vines,
rocks, and other parts of Ma's garden. To this heap, Beidermann
sets a match, and the twins dance around the sudden shiny flame,
itself unseen in the bright sun, to stamp out wayward sparks;
their oil-soaked trousers, shirts and hair severely imperiled.

Earnest at his work, Beidermann pours another dose of coal
oil into his machine, and swings it about to take a new swath.
He seems set to do this as long as anyone will allow him.

He swings his horses around at the garden's end, and I walk
to meet them, the mounds of insects flickering away from their
hooves like splashed water. I wave Beidermann to a halt. He is
puffing, he wipes his face—this pursuit of ephemera is a heavy
business. But I do not wish to be insulting to his efforts. I point
to the meager contents of his scraper.

It works a little, I say. But not enough.

Beidermann studies the poverty of his haul with a squinting
eye, and I cannot tell by his look if he knows the measure of
his foolishness. But he is not the Beidermann we know if he
cannot tell me why it is a famous triumph.

Yaas, he slowly allows. Not so many hoppers, true, but I am
scraping up the eggs these little bastards leave, and saving you
from going through this again in another month.

If they can find anything left in a month, says I, they are
welcome to it. Take a look. Does this look like there will be a
single growing thing for a God-damned bug to eat, let alone a
man and his wife and boys?

This is more anger than I mean to show—but why should I
hide it? Beidermann looks away, then curls the ends of his reins
around his machine's handles.

Well, what I am trying to do here, he says, is give you a
hand.

Lloyd Zimpel

Sure enough, I say. And I will say that I appreciate your intentions. But when you go to experimenting with your machines, you might think to do it on your own place—I say this knowing he has escaped the scourge—there is no need to come here and play with me.

Here, here, says Beidermann, who is not likely to misperceive that the cause of my ire is as much his good fortune as my bad. These bastards have not come down on me, at least not yet, as you well know. This thing is an experiment. I meant to help.

Am I to tell him how he can finally help? Am I to say he must feel the burden of misfortunes of his own for once; that he needs a few failures under his belt and then I will shake his hand? My own pettiness galls me; begrudging another's happy lot; but I am exasperated, too; more than that overwhelmed by flood, fire, drouth, cattle gone down in storms, blight, a family more miserable than not, often; and now this devastation of insects. And it chose to pass Beidermann by, so he comes with his toy to play with those laid waste.

To be sure, says I. But you might think about confining your experiments to the Widow Jenssen and do not come here with any fool devices!

It surprises me a little, how hard these words come out; for I feel no push to reduce the proud Beidermann. He does not bring his machine to tease me, I know; he tells the truth there. But I am not Job, and when afflictions descend upon a man and he heaves to free himself, even a little, his lashing about may aggrieve others, as here Beidermann.

But if Beidermann is stung, he is not humbled. He slaps at the grasshoppers; his horses stomp, their harness rattling, and Beidermann comes around their tossing heads, close up to me, a blackness deep in his eyes, his coarse lips drawn down, and pokes the half-finger on his right hand to my breast. Yet his voice is mild enough, as if the matter he addresses, for all its consequence to others, is not so filled with importance to a man of parts such as himself.

As I remember his words, they start like a sermon: For all the years you have lived, old man, he says, I guess you have still not learned what you should. For God-damned sure, you have not come across a fellow like myself, who if he is going to fool with you—if he is going to *play* with you—why, then everybody in the country is going to know it. Let me tell you: I figured this tin thing would do a job against these bugs—he bats them aside—and if it did not turn out that way, well, I regret it, and you have my apology for it.

The twins crowd my elbows as he speaks, as if to urge me to take Beidermann's apology. These two know more of Beidermann than any of us, by way of their months tagging in his wake, trapping, herding, milking, butchering, wood-cutting, well-digging, fishing, killing, skinning. They eye him, me, Henry, Otto, Harris, uneasily. They know what in Beidermann is simple aggravation, irritation, anger or killing rage; and what they see now I cannot tell from their faces—and for a long time I have been uncertain whether they have come to weigh heavier on Beidermann's side than my own.

So you have mistaken me badly, says Beidermann. But I am not one to take it as too serious a matter, because a man has to keep in mind how hard you have been hit. All this time with no rain, and then these critters come down on you hardest of all.

I nod full assent. But suddenly we have another voice, and it is Harris, the last of my boys I would choose to speak for me in any dispute.

Yes, that is true, Harris throws in loudly, having come up, shovel in hand, on Beidermann's other side, and while more than a match for him in scowls he altogether lacks our neighbor's mild tone of reason. On his neck the strawberry mark is redder than usual—a bad sign.

He says: You bet the bastards have damn well hit us hardest of all, sure. But there is some they have not hit at all, and a suspicious man might want to know why that is, eh? A suspicious man and a dumb enough one, might be persuaded to ask himself a stupid question: What's this? Old *Bittermilk* did not shoo them over here, did he, eh? We can all have a good laugh at that dumb idea, can we not, eh?

Harris reaches out that big hand—they are all big-handed, these boys of mine, the grown ones, and the twins promise that way too, big of arm, big of body, the worst of it being that Harris, while biggest of any but Otto, is smallest in well-balanced judgment, even as he is biggest of all in temper; and far too big a complainer, too much a grumbler, a dour man, grown from a heavy-hearted boy; for all that when he ran bare-footed, Ma prodded him toward the cheerful ways of his brothers; her joking and stories the others prized, while he stared down and kicked at the dirt. . . . His big hand sweeps out and plucks up one of the mass of passing grasshoppers. This he holds pinched by its wings at arm's length toward Beidermann.

Recognize this feller, do ye? he says: he could be addressing the insect or the man.

With a flick of his hand Beidermann slaps the thing away—to him it is not the insult Harris intended—and he says: That little insect has more brains than you do.

It is this, I suspect, something rotten like this, that Harris hankers after, by way of proving up his sneering view of Beidermann, and also to fill his need to run a course counter to his brothers'. There is a black streak in him, as Ma has always said, laying it to a spooked element in her Klaus bloodlines; in that her grandfather, dead before she knew him, left a legacy of bloody wildness across the south of Indiana, the cause of it, as her relatives tell the story, pure inborn cussedness. A singular man with a singular appearance: a three-inch strawberry mark on his cheek—not on his neck—upon which the whiskers he grew abundantly elsewhere would not take. Mean to man and beast equally, it is said, he died murdered after long misuse of his wife and children and relatives of all description: Knifed to death, he was, with praise and no reckoning for the murderer, his young son. . . .

But these are different times and a man must show some judgment in the way he lives his life among others; for he encounters too many in every aspect of living not to take into account their sensibilities, as Harris is not willing to do, or able to do. And perhaps a little of that lack is in Beidermann too, for all that he can better accommodate his inward self than can my reckless son; Beidermann, the sweating outward hulk of him, shoulders sloped, and grasshoppers flitting past with the sound of crystals in an ice storm.

We are all in this picture. The twins turn in agony, and Otto yells to Harris to put down the shovel; and Ma calling him back to finish his furrow as if he had simply tarried to get a drink. And my own schoolmarmish admonition, no more suitable to the circumstance:

You lay off this rough talk, you two. . . .

Beidermann looks at me down his grand nose, as though to say: Old man, it is late in the game to be teaching your son manners, while Harris, drawn by rage down his own blind path, hears not so much as a mouse's squeak of caution, as he steps up to raise his shovel.

He has more brains than me, does he, then? he says into Beidermann's face. Well, he God-damned well has more b-s than you, you sorry excuse for a dog's p-k!

Ah! Beidermann must be given this: he does not appear to have been called names by enough men for it to be commonplace, but he does not flinch or blink, although I cannot say the same for myself; and Ma utters a throaty sigh, while Beidermann stands cool as a man without fear or concern. . . . Indeed, he can see there is call for neither—for Otto steps forward and in one big motion wraps Harris around from behind, long arms clamping down like a vise; so there will be no swinging shovel, indeed, no hostile move at all, no move of any sort, for, straining only slightly, Otto removes his younger brother an inch off the ground and swivels around so the two face away from Beidermann; Harris puffing and blustering the while over his shoulder as I step up to loosen the shovel from his pinned hand. He is purple with choler, and kicks back at his brother, who shows us a nimble dance among the grasshoppers to keep his shins undamaged. But Otto is much the stronger boy, and all Harris' inflamed exertion is unavailing, for he is soundly snared. Indeed, there is enough in him still sensible, so that he does not struggle to the degree that Otto need hurt him, as he hops him like a frog some yards away, close to the plow's handles, saying: I am going to tie you down to this plow, if you do not stop this horses-t behavior!

Yaas! calls Beidermann. Hitch the bugger to it and let him plow a few acres, to work some sense into him!

Harris, I would think, in his heightened state could almost do it. But there is no fight now, nor promise of one, and no call for taunts and jibes from either party. I step into Beidermann's way.

This is a sorry business, I say to him. I would never want to see it, and I know you are man enough to recognize it all as a mistake on my boy's part. It is not the way we do business with our neighbors, but this is a time when we are badly pushed, as you know.

Beidermann sizes me up. Yes, you can say that if you want to, old man, he says, calling me that again, which he has not done before today, this uncommon day, so his mockery is clear. But I am bound to see it my own way, and I will say this: your boy there knows where my fence lines are, and all he has to do is cross them one time, and I will show him the ways I do business with my neighbors when they do not show any more sense than he does.

He unhooks his team's traces from his device and backs the team to the singletrees of his wagon, hitches up, and heaves the tin sheet onto it. Dirt and oil and the few grasshoppers still in it sail off in a ribbon, the greasiness of the mess catching a brief rainbow glimmer of sun.

We watch that, and we watch Beidermann. It is our tableau in the yard under the ugly noon sun: the grasshoppers form a landscape, and out of the dust of it arise their stridulations, a gibing chorus to the slap of our hands. The twins watch tormented as the pillar Beidermann is carried from them by their brother's foolish enmity; and as Beidermann yanks the fly-screens off his horses' heads, they look to Harris as if he may have it in him to offer a decent word and set things right; and they look to Ma as if she might smooth the rough business over with a piece of pie and cup of coffee; and they look to me...how? Perhaps as if I might haul myself up like Moses and deliver a pronouncement so wise, so profound, so all-embracing in the comfort it laves over all, that the sweaty lot of us will stagger into each other's arms, crying out our folly.... And the twins are off trapping weasels with Beidermann tomorrow....

But what if I misread their look, and it is not hope that is in it, but instead only the censure of ten-year-old boys? And better it be censure than hope. Here, under the parching sun, amidst the awful insects, their hope, their lack of it, their very hope of hope, matters not at all. What room is there for a child's faith here? What expectation of joy reasonable in this blight?

I smolder, yes. Beidermann even at peace is not an easy man to swallow, and we have him here rampant; and it cannot be, we cannot have a wrathful neighbor, or else we look to another war across the fence lines—and of those this country has seen enough, lastly by the bellicose Krupp with his neighbor to the North, Bruntz; their dispute over a ditch that one of them dug—Krupp is that last man to make clear which—and thus diverted the limb of Skunk Creek that crosses each property. Who was right and who was wrong in that dispute remains unknown, although shots were fired in the night, fat-bellied Krupp told me while maintaining himself an unlikely innocent victim; although Bruntz, like the slop-bucket Dutchman he was, had not sense enough to make his side heard, and in short time was busted and gone—back to the wife's folks in Wisconsin, no doubt; and from the poor look of his place he was headed there soon enough with or without Krupp's vagrant ditches and skulking midnight potshots. . . .

Otto takes his hold off Harris' shoulder but stands beside him close as a prison guard, and Beidermann sets one foot on a horizontal spoke of his wagon wheel and swings himself up to the bench. The twins come up, as if they might wave him off down the lane and run behind in the dust for a little way, as they sometimes do. They wait, their faces desolate.

Stepping up, I lay one hand on the big rump of Beidermann's mare, slapping grasshoppers off it, and take a bead up the reins to Beidermann's face; but before I can offer any moderate word, Beidermann speaks:

If you like the feel of my horse's a-s, old man, he says, maybe you would like mine, too. Well, I can make it available for kissing by that red-faced boy of yours.

For that one moment I am willing to give up on the insolent Beidermann. There are several of us here who in two minutes can render the smart fellow, for all his size and muscle, such a lesson for his sass as he will record in his memoirs. Should I be ashamed to say it? I could have set the boys on him like dogs, the twins alone holding back. . . . And then we are all barbarians again. If I am a Christian man, as I am, then I know where I stand here: no case for turning the other cheek was ever better made, a school-book example, quite as if the Almighty Himself had hand-fashioned it expressly as a test—should the drouth and grasshoppers be insufficient—by way of showing His floundering servant how fragile is the stitching of one's faith, how near the surface, weakness.

Beidermann, Beidermann, I call to him, haughty on his wagon seat. This is no good. I can see I am too hasty in my criticism of you. I know your intention is neighborly. But it is these damned bugs. They will kill everything alive, and friendship and neighborliness are included in the victims, and I cannot abide to see us taken in by the effect of them. Beidermann, we have all had a bad season—But there I stop, for Beidermann has not had a bad season.

Now he hoists the reins above the swinging tails of his team and measures me with a coal-black eye.

Bugs are bugs, he says. The bugs will go, but I will still be here. It was not bugs that give me hard words. It was your boy there. He pokes his bristled chin at Harris, who growls as if he is a damned dog, and slaps the reins lightly on the horses' backs, dislodging a few dozen grasshoppers, and the team steps out.

Harris bawls some last word—I am so fed up with him I cannot listen—and Otto, much provoked, shoves him back; and Beidermann's rig departs down the ruts of our road in an eddy of dust and grasshoppers, his contraption rattling loudly in the wagon bed. Tears start in the twins' eyes; they try to look at me but cannot; and Ma shakes her head back and forth, pursing her lips and looking at me and shaking her head. Presently, Otto retrieves Harris' shovel, hands it to him, and heads to the bar, saying: The son of a bitch could at least take his bugs with him. . . .

Aug. 20. . . . By the afternoon they are mostly gone, and at milking time, when I walk to the barn, it is without the dismal crunch underfoot. One by one, two by two, they have picked up and sailed away. Obeying what signal? What signal needed beyond the ravished landscape they have left us? Holes in the ground where onions grew, fork-handles filigreed, barren box-elders, a half-dozen hens dead of gluttony and the eggs of others too bug-laced for eating except by the stuffed and sleeping hogs; a little of the garden is saved by the hides, Ma's geraniums wilted but alive under the holey quilts. Look, says Henry at the barn door, you can see a half-mile in any direction before there is anything but gray.

Not every one has flown. A few hold back, so attached are they to our largess, in the house a few, still. . . . One straggler now creeps toward my lamp—to fatten on the oil, perhaps, to consume the very flame, to bring us news of the unregenerate Beidermann; this specimen no less brash than our neighbor, choosing to rest saucily before my lamp, a hand's breadth from my pen, unaware of the hatred mantling in me. By my tablet the creature stands unmoving, then quivers, coarsely adjusts his stiff and gauzy wings, and tucks in his drumstick legs as if readying them for use. For all his diminutive size he is not dainty, but crude, his aspect rank, his single adornment the pearls of light caught on the sawteeth on the backs of his legs. His buffalo head is all eye and jaw: He faces me straight on, undaunted by my moving pen, although his feelers poke up alert, twitching one way and another, eyes fixed. He does not see what I am but senses it. If I turn my hand quickly to the side, it will crush him—for that feeble plate of armor across his back protects him in his world, but not in mine. Or is that my mistake, and it is indeed his world?

Lloyd Zimpel is the author of numerous short stories and a novel, *Meeting the Bear*.

"HEY, OVER HERE! I'M THIS YEAR'S
PAGE TURNER."

BLACK SWANS / *Lauren Slater*

T HERE IS SOMETHING SATISFYING and scary about making an angel, lowering your bulky body into the drowning fluff, stray flakes landing on your face. I am seven or eight and the sky looms above me, grey and dead. I move my arms and legs— expanding, contracting—sculpting snow before it can swallow me up. I feel the cold filter into my head, seep through the wool of my mittens. I swish wider, faster, then roll out of my mould to inspect its form. There is the imprint of my head, my arms which have swelled into white wings. I step back, step forward, pause and peer. Am I dead or alive down there? Is this a picture of heaven or hell? I am worried about where I will go when I die, that each time I swallow an invisible stone will get caught in my throat. I worry that when I eat a plum, a tree will grow in my belly, its branches twining around my bones, choking. When I walk through a door I must tap the frame three times. Between each nighttime prayer to Yahweh I close my eyes and count to ten and a half.

And now I look down at myself sketched in the snow. A familiar anxiety chews at the edges of my heart, even while I notice the beauty of the white fur on all the trees, the reverent silence of this season. I register a mistake on my angel, what looks like a thumbprint on its left wing. I reach down to erase it, but unable to smooth the snow perfectly, I start again on another angel, lowering myself, swishing and sweeping, rolling over—no. Yet another mistake, this time the symmetry in the wingspan wrong. A compulsion comes over me. I do it again, and again. In my memory hours go by. My fingers inside my mittens get wrinkled and raw. My breath comes heavily and the snow begins to blue. A moon rises, a perfect crescent pearl whose precise shape I will never be able to recreate. I ache for something I cannot name. Someone calls me, a mother or a father. *Come in now, come in now.* Very early the next morning I awaken, look out my bedroom window, and see the yard covered with my frantic forms—hundreds of angels, none of them quite right. The forms twist and strain, the wings seeming to struggle up in the winter sun, as if each angel were longing for escape, for a free flight that might crack the crystal and ice of her still, stiff world.

Looking back on it now, I think maybe those moments in the snow were when my OCD began, although it didn't come to me full-fledged until my mid-twenties. OCD stands for obsessive-compulsive disorder, and some studies say over three million Americans suffer from it. The "it" is not the commonplace rituals that weave throughout so many of our lives—the woman who checks the stove a few times before she leaves for work, or the man who combs his bangs back, and then again, seeking symmetry. obsessive-compulsive disorder is pervasive and extreme, inundating the person's life to the point where normal functioning becomes difficult, maybe even impossible.

For a long time my life was difficult but not impossible. Both in my childhood and my adulthood I'd suffered from various psychiatric ailments—depressions especially—but none of these were as surreal and absurd as the obsessive-compulsive disorder that one day presented itself. Until I was twenty-five or so, I don't think I could have been really diagnosed with OCD, although my memory of the angels indicates I had tendencies in that direction. I was a child at once nervous and bold, a child who loved trees that trickled sap, the Vermont fields where grass grew the color of deep-throated rust. I was a child who gathered earthworms, the surprising pulse of pink on my fingers, and yet these same fingers, later in the evening, came to prayer points, searching for safety in the folds of my sheets, in the quick counting rituals.

Some mental health professionals claim that the onset of obsession is a response to an underlying fear, a recent trauma, say, or a loss. I don't believe that is always true because, no matter how hard I think about it, I remember nothing unusual or disorienting before my first attack, three years out of college. I don't know exactly why at two o'clock one Saturday afternoon what felt like a seizure shook me. I recall lying in my apartment in Cambridge. The floors were painted blue, the curtains a sleepy white. They bellied in and out with the breezes. I was immersed in a book, *The Seven Story Mountain,* walking my way through the tale's church, dabbing holy water on my forehead. A priest was crooning. A monk moaned. And suddenly this: A thought careening across my cortex. I CAN'T CONCENTRATE. Of course the thought disturbed my concentration, and the monk's moan turned into a whisper, disappeared.

I blinked, looked up. I was back in Cambridge on a blue floor. The blue floor suddenly frightened me; between the planks I could see lines of dark dirt, and the sway of a spider crawling. Let me get back, I thought, into the world of the book. I lowered my eyes to the page, but instead of being able to see the print, there was the thought blocking out all else: I CAN'T CONCENTRATE.

Now I started to panic. Each time I tried to get back to the book the words crumbled, lost their sensible shapes. I said to myself *I must not allow that thought about concentration to come into my mind anymore*, but, of course, the more I tried to suppress it, the louder it jangled. I looked at my hand. I ached for its familiar skin, the paleness of its palm and the three threaded lines that had been with me since birth, but as I held it out before my eyes, the phrase I CAN'T CONCENTRATE ON MY HAND blocked out my hand, so all I saw was a blur of flesh giving way to the bones beneath, and inside the bones the grimy marrow, and in the grimy marrow the individual cells, all disconnected. Shattered skin.

My throat closed up with terror. For surely if I'd lost the book, lost language, lost flesh, I was well on my way to losing the rest of the world. And all because of a tiny phrase that forced me into a searing self-consciousness, that plucked me from the moment into the meta-moment so I was doomed to think about thinking instead of thinking other thoughts. My mind devouring my mind.

I tried to force my brain onto other topics but with each mental dodge I became aware that I was dodging, and each time I itched I became aware that I was itching, and with each inhalation I became aware that I was inhaling, and I thought *if I think too much about breathing, will I forget how to breathe?*

I ran into the bathroom. There was a strange pounding in my head, and then a sensation I can only describe as a hiccup of the brain. My brain seemed to be seizing as the phrase about concentration jerked across it. I delved into the medicine cabinet, found a bottle of aspirin, took three, stood by the sink for five minutes. No go. Delved again, pulled out another bottle—Ativan, a Valium-like medication belonging to my housemate Adam. Another five minutes, my brain still squirting. One more Ativan, a tiny white triangle that would put me to sleep. I would sleep this strange spell off, wake up me again, sane again. I went back to my bed. The day darkened. The Ativan spread through my system. Lights in a neighboring window seemed lonely and sweet. I saw the shadow of a bird in a tree, and it had angel wings, and it soared me someplace else, its call a pure cry.

"What's wrong with you?" he said, shaking my shoulder. My housemate Adam stood over me, his face a blur. Through cracked eyelids I saw a wavering world, none of its outlines resolved: the latticed shadow of a tree on a white wall, my friend's face a streak of pink. I am O.K. I thought, for this was what waking up was always like, the gentle resurfacing. I sat up, looked around.

"You've been sleeping for hours and hours," he said. "You slept from yesterday afternoon until now."

I reached up, gently touched a temple. I felt the far-away nip of my pulse. My pulse was there. I was here.

"Weird day yesterday," I said. I spoke slowly, listening to my words, testing them on my tongue. So far so good.

I stood up. "You look weird," he said, "unsteady."

"I'm O.K.," I said, and then, in that instant, a surge of anxiety. I had lied. I had not been O.K. *Say God I'm sorry fourteen times* I ordered myself. *This is crazy* I said to myself. *Fifteen times* a voice from somewhere else seemed to command. "You really all right?" Adam asked. I closed my eyes, counted, blinked back open.

"O.K.," I said. "I'm going to shower."

But it wasn't O.K.. As soon as I was awake, obsessive thoughts returned. What before had been inconsequential behaviors like counting to three before I went through a doorway or checking the stove several times before bed, now became imperatives. There were a thousand and one of them to follow: rules about how to step, what it meant to touch my mouth, a hot consuming urge to fix the crooked angles of the universe. It was constant, a cruel nattering. *There, that tilted picture on the wall. Scratch your head with your left hand only.* It was noise, the beak of a woodpecker in the soft bark of my brain. But the worst, by far, were the dread thoughts about concentrating. I picked up a book but couldn't read, so aware was I of myself reading, and the fear of that awareness, for it meant a cold disconnection from this world.

I began to avoid written language because of the anxiety associated with words. I stopped reading. Every sentence I wrote came out only half coherent. I became afraid of pens and paper, the red felt tip bleeding into white, a wound. What was it? What was I? I could not recognize myself spending hours counting, checking, avoiding. Gods seemed to hover in their air, inhabit me, blowing me full of their strange stellar breaths. I wanted my body back. Instead I pulsed and stuttered and sparked with a glow not my own.

I spent the next several weeks mostly in my bedroom, door closed, shades drawn. I didn't want to go out because any movement might set off a cycle of obsessions. I sat hunched and lost weight. My friend Adam, who had some anxiety problems of his own and was a real pooh-pooher of "talk therapy," found me a behaviorist at McClean.

"These sorts of conditions," the behavioral psychologist, Dr. Lipman, told me as I sat one day in his office, "are associated with people who have depressive temperaments, but, unlike depression, they do not yield particularly well to more traditional modes of psychotherapy. We have, however, had some real success with cognitive/behavioral treatments."

Outside it was a shining summer day. His office was dim though, his blinds adjusted so only tiny gold chinks of light sprinkled through, illuminating him in patches. He was older, maybe fifty, and pudgy, and had tufts of hair in all the wrong places, in the whorls of his ears and his nostrils. I had a bad feeling about him.

Nevertheless, he was all I had right now. "What is this sort of condition exactly?" I asked. My voice, whenever I spoke these days, seemed slowed, stuck, words caught in my throat. I had to keep touching my throat, four times, five times, six times, or I would be punished by losing the power of speech all together.

"Obsessive-compulsive disorder," he announced. "Only you," he said, and lifted his chin a little proudly, "have an especially difficult case of it."

This, of course, was not what I wanted to hear. "What's so especially difficult about my case?" I asked.

He tapped his chin with the eraser end of his pencil. He sat back in his leather seat. When the wind outside blew, the gold chinks scattered across his face and desk. Suddenly, the world cleared a bit. The papers on his desk seemed animated, rustling, sheaves full of wings, books full of birds. I felt creepy, despondent, and excited all at once. Maybe he could help me. Maybe he had some special knowledge.

He then went on to explain to me how most people with obsessive thoughts—*my hands are filthy*—for instance, always follow those thoughts with a compulsive behavior, like handwashing. And while I did have some compulsive behaviors, Dr. Lipman explained, I also reported that my most distressing obsession had to do with concentration, and that the concentration obsession had no clear-cut compulsion following in its wake.

"Therefore," he said. His eyes sparkled as he spoke. He seemed excited by my case. He seemed so sure of himself that for a moment I was back with language again, only this time it was his language, his words forming me.

"Therefore you are what we call a primary ruminator!"

A cow, I thought, chewing and chewing on the floppy scum of its cud. I lowered my head.

He went on to tell me about treatment obstacles. Supposedly "primary ruminators" are especially challenging because, while you can train people to cease compulsive behaviors, you can't train them nearly as easily to tether their thoughts. His method, he told me, would be to use a certain instrument to desensitize me to the obsessive thought, to teach me not to be afraid of it so, when it entered my mind, I wouldn't panic and thereby set off a whole cycle of anxiety and its partner, avoidance.

"How will we do it?" I asked.

And that is when he pulled "the instrument" from his desk drawer, a Walkman with a tiny tape in it. He told me he'd used it with people who were similar to me. He told me I was to record my voice saying "I can't concentrate I can't concentrate" and then wear the Walkman playing my own voice back to me for at least two hours a day. Soon, he said, I'd become so used to the thought it would no longer bother me.

He looked over at the clock. About half the session had gone by. "We still have twenty more minutes," he said, pressing the red recorder button, holding the miniature microphone up to my mouth. "Why don't you start speaking now."

I paid Dr. Lipman for the session, borrowed the Walkman and the tape, and then left, stepping into the summer light. McClean is a huge stately hospital, buildings with pillars, yawning lawns. The world outside looked lazy in the sweet heat of June. Tulips in the garden lapped at the pollen-rich air with black tongues. A squirrel chirped high in the tuft of a tree. For a moment the world seemed lovely. Then, from far across the lawn, I saw a shadow in a window. Drawn for a reason I could not articulate, I stepped closer, and closer still. The shadow resolved itself into lines—two dark brows, a nose. A girl, pressed against glass on a top-floor ward. Her hands were fisted on either side of her face, her curls in a ratty tangle. Her mouth was open, and though I could not hear her, I saw the red splash of her scream.

Behavior therapy is in some ways the antithesis of psychoanalysis. Psychoanalysis focuses on cause, behavior therapy on consequence. Although I've always been a critic of old-style psychoanalysis with its fetish for the past, I don't completely discount the importance of origins. And I have always believed in the mind as an entity that at once subsumes the body and radiates beyond it, and therefore in need of interventions surpassing the mere technical; interventions that whisper to mystery, stroke the soul.

The Walkman, however, was a completely technical intervention. It had little red studs for buttons. The tape whirred efficiently in its center like a slick dark heart. My own voice echoed back to me, all blips and snaky static. I wondered what the obsession with concentration meant. Surely it had some significance beyond the quirks in my own neuronal wiring. Surely the neuron itself—that tiny pulse of life embedded in the brain's lush banks—was a god-given charge. When I was a girl, I had seen stalks of wheat filled with a strange red light. When I was a girl, I once peeled back the corn's green clasps to find yellow pearls. With the Walkman on, I closed my eyes, saw again the prongs of corn, the wide world, and myself floating out of that world, in a place above all planets, severed even from my own mind. And I knew the obsession had something to do with deep disconnection and too much awe.

"There may be no real reasons," Dr. Lipman repeated to me during my next visit. "OCD could well be the result of a nervous system that's too sensitive. If the right medication is ever developed, we would use that."

Because the right medication had not yet been found, I wore the Walkman. The earplugs felt spongy. Sometimes I wore it to bed, listening to my own voice repeat the obsessive fear. When I took the earphones off the silence was complete. My sheets were damp from sweat. I waited. Shadows whirled around. Planets sent down their lights, laying them across the blue floor. Blue. Silver. Space. *I can't concentrate.*

I did very little for the next year. Dr. Lipman kept insisting I wear the Walkman, turning up the volume, keeping it on for three, now four hours at a time. Fear and grief prevented me from eating much. When I was too terrified to get out of bed, Dr. Lipman checked me into the local hospital, where I lay amidst IV drips, bags of blood, murmuring heart machines that let me know someone somewhere near was still alive.

It was in the hospital that I was first introduced to psychiatric medications, which the doctors tried me on to no avail. The medications had poetic names and frequently rhymed with one another—Nortriptyline, Desipramine, Amitriptyline. Nurses brought me capsules in miniature paper cups, or oblong shapes of white that left a salty tingle on my tongue. None of them worked, except to make me drowsy and dull.

And then one day Dr. Lipman said to me, "there's a new medication called Prozac, still in its trial period, but it's seventy-percent effective with OCD. I want to send you to a Dr. Vuckovic, here at McClean. He's one of the physicians doing trial runs."

I shrugged, willing to try. I'd tried so much, surely this couldn't hurt. I didn't expect much though. I certainly didn't expect what I finally got.

In my memory, Vuckovic is the Prozac Doctor. He has an office high in the eaves of McClean. His desk gleams. His children smile out from frames lined up behind him. In the corner is a computer with a screensaver of hypnotic swirling stars. I watch the stars die and swell. I watch the simple gold band on Vuckovic's hand. For a moment I think that maybe in here I'll finally be able to escape the infected repetitions of my own mind. And then I hear a clock tick-tick-ticking. The sound begins to bother me; I cannot tune it out. "The clock is ruining my concentration," I think and turn toward it. The numbers on its face are not numbers but tiny painted pills, green and white. A chime hangs down, with another capsule, probably a plastic replica, swinging from the end of it. Back. Forth. Back. Back.

The pads of paper on Vuckovic's desk are all edged in green and white, with the word "Prozac" scripted across the bottom. The pen has "Prozac" embossed in tiny letters. He asks me about my symptoms for a few minutes, and then uses the Prozac pen to write out a prescription.

"What about side effects?" I ask.

"Very few," the Prozac Doctor answers. He smiles. "Maybe some queasiness. A headache in the beginning. Some short-term insomnia. All in all it's a very good medication. The safest we have."

"Behavior therapy hasn't helped," I say. I feel I'm speaking slowly, for the sound of that clock is consuming me. I put my hands over my ears.

"What is it?" he asks.

"Your—clock."

He looks toward it.

"Would you mind putting it away?"

"Then I would be colluding with your disease," he says. "If I put the clock away, you'll just fixate on something else."

"Disease," I repeat. "I have a disease."

"Without doubt," he says. "OCD can be a crippling disease, but now, for the first time, we have the drugs to combat it."

I take the prescription and leave. I will see him in one month for a follow-up. Disease. Combat. Collusions. My mind, it seems, is my enemy, my illness an absurdity that has to be exterminated. I believe this. The treatment I'm receiving, with its insistence upon cure— which means the abolition of hurt instead of its transformation— helps me to believe this. I have, indeed, been invaded by a virus, a germ I need to rid myself of.

Looking back on it now, I see this belief only added to my panic, shrunk my world still smaller.

On the first day of Prozac I felt nothing, on the second and third nausea, and then for the rest of that week headaches so intense I wanted to groan and lower my face into a bowl of crushed ice. I had never had migraines before. In their own way they are beautiful, all pulsing suns and squeezing colors. When I closed my eyes, pink shapes flapped and angels' halos spun. I was a girl again, lying in the snow. Slowly, one by one, the frozen forms lifted toward the light.

And then there really was an angel over me, pressing a cool cloth to my forehead. He held two snowy tablets out to me, and in a haze of pain I took them.

"You'll be all right," Adam said to me. When I cried it was a creek coming from my eyes.

I rubbed my eyes. The headache ebbed.

"How are you?" he asked.

"O.K.," I said. And waited for a command. *Touch your nose, blink twelve times, try not to think about think about concentrating.*

The imperatives came—I could hear them—but from far far away, like birds beyond a mountain, a sound nearly silent and easy to ignore.

"I'm...O.K.." I repeated. I went out into the kitchen. The clock on the stove ticked. I pressed my ear against it and heard, this time, a steady, almost soothing pulse.

Most things, I think, diminish over time, rock and mountain, glacier and bone. But this wasn't the nature of Prozac, or me on Prozac. One day I was ill, cramped up with fears, and the next day the ghosts were gone. Imagine having for years a raging fever, and then one day someone hands you a new kind of pill, and within a matter of hours sweat dries, the scarlet swellings go down, your eyes no longer burn. The grass appears green again, the sky a gentle blue. *Hello hello. Remember me?* the planet whispers.

But to say I returned to the world is even a bit misleading, for all my life the world has seemed off-kilter. On Prozac, not only did the acute obsessions dissolve; so too did the blander depression that had been with me since my earliest memories. A sense of immense calm flooded me. Colors came out, yellow leaping from the light where it had long lain trapped, greens unwinding from the grass, dusk letting loose its lavender.

By the fourth day I still felt so shockingly fine that I called the Prozac Doctor. I pictured him in his office, high in the eaves of McClean. I believed he had saved me. He loomed large.

"I'm well," I told him.

"Not yet. It takes at least a month to build up a therapeutic blood level."

"No," I said. "It doesn't." I felt a rushing joy. "The medicine you gave me has made me well. I've, I've actually never felt better."

A pause on the line. "I suppose it could be possible."

"Yes," I said. "It's happened."

I became a "happening" kind of person. Peter Kramer, author of *Listening to Prozac* has written extensively on the drug's ability to galvanize personality change as well as to soothe fears or elevate mood. Kramer calls Prozac a cosmetic medication, for it seems to re-shape the psyche, lift the face of the soul.

One night, soon after the medication had "kicked in," I sat at the kitchen table with Adam. He was stuck in the muck of his master's thesis, fearful of failure.

"It's easy," I said. "Break the project down into bits. A page a day. Six days, one chapter. Twelve days, two. One month, presto." I snapped my fingers. "You're finished."

Adam looked at me, said nothing. The kitchen grew quiet, a deliberate sort of silence he seemed to be purposefully manufacturing so I could hear the echo of my own voice. Bugs thumped on the screen. I heard the high happy pitch of a cheerleader, the sensible voice of a vocational counselor. In a matter of moments I had gone from a fumbling, unsure person to this—all pragmatism, all sure solutions. For the first time on Prozac I felt afraid.

I lay in bed that night. From the next room I heard the patter of Adam's typewriter keys. He was stuck in the mire, inching forward and falling back. Where was I; who was I? I lifted my hand to my face, the same motion as before, when the full force of obsession had struck me. The hand was still unfamiliar, but wonderfully so now, the three threaded lines seams of silver, the lights from passing cars rotating on my walls like the swish of a spaceship softly landing.

In space I was then, wondering. How could a drug change my mind so abruptly? How could it bring forth buried or new parts of my personality? The oldest questions, I know. My brain wasn't wet clay and paste, as all good brains should be, but a glinting thing crossed with wires. I wasn't human but machine. No, I wasn't machine, but animal, linked to my electrified biology more completely than I could have imagined. We have come to think, lately, of machines and animals, of machines and nature, as occupying opposite sides of the spectrum—there is IBM and then there's the lake—but really they are so similar. A computer goes on when you push its button. A gazelle goes on when it sees a lynx. Only humans are supposedly different, above the pure cause and effect of the hard-wired, primitive world. Free will and all.

But no, maybe not. For I had swallowed a pill designed through technology, and in doing so, I was discovering myself embedded in an animal world. I was a purely chemical being, mood and personality seeping through serotonin. We are all taught to believe it's true, but how strange to feel that supposed truth bubbling right in your own tweaked brainpan. Who was I, all skin and worm; all herd? For the next few weeks, amidst feelings of joy and deep relief, these thoughts accompanied me, these slow, simmering misgivings. In dreams, beasts roamed the rafters of my bones, and my bones were twined with wire, teeth tiny silicone chips.

I went to Drumlin Farm one afternoon to see the animals. A goose ate grass in an imperturbable rhythm. Sheep brayed robotically, their noses pointing toward the sky. I reached out to touch their fur. Simmering misgivings, yes, but my fingers alive, feeling clumps of cream, of wool.

Every noon I took my pill. Instead of just placing it on my tongue and swallowing with water, I unscrewed the capsule. White powder poured into my hands. I tossed the plastic husk away, cradled the healing talc. I tasted it, a burst of bitterness, a gagging. I took it that way every day, the silky slide of Prozac powder, the harshness in my mouth.

Mornings now, I got up early to jog, showered efficiently, then strode off to the library. I was able to go back to work, cutting deli part-time at Formaggio's while I prepared myself for Divinity School the next year by reading. I read with an appetite, hungry from all the time I'd lost to illness. The pages of the book seemed very white; the words were easy, black beads shining, ebony in my quieted mind.

I found a book in the library's medical section about obsessive-compulsive disorder. I sat in a corner, on a corduroy cushion, to read it. And there, surrounded by pages and pages on the nature of God and mystery, on Job who cried out at his unfathomable pain, I read about my disorder from a medical perspective, followed the charts and graphs and correlation coefficients. The author proposed that OCD was solely physical in origin, and had the same neurological etiology as Tourettes. Obsessive symptoms, the author suggested, are atavistic responses left over from primitive grooming behaviors. We still have the ape in us; a bird flies in our blood. The obsessive person, linked to her reptilian roots, her mammalian ancestors, cannot stop picking parasites off her brother's back, combing her hair with her tongue, or doing the human equivalent of nest building, picking up stick after stick, leaf after leaf, until her bloated home sit ridiculously unstable in the crotch of an old oak tree.

Keel keel the crow in me cries. The pig grunts. The screen of myself blinks on. Blinks off. Darkens.

Still, I was mostly peaceful, wonderfully organized. My mind felt lubed, thoughts slipping through so easily, words bursting into bloom. I was reminded of being a girl, on the island of Barbados where we once vacationed. My father took me to a banquet beneath a tropical Basian sky. Greased black men slithered under low poles, their liquid bodies bending to meet the world. Torches flared, and on a long table before me steamed food of every variety. *A feast* my father said, *all the good things in life*. Yes, that was what Prozac was first like for me—all the good things in life—roasted ham, delicate grilled fish, lemon halves wrapped in yellow waxed paper, fat plums floating in jars.

I could, I thought, do anything in this state of mind. I put my misgivings aside (how fast they would soon come back; how hard they would hit) and ate into my days, a long banquet. I did things I'd never done before, swimming at dawn in Walden Pond, writing poetry I knew was bad, and loving it anyway.

I applied for and was awarded a three-month grant to go to Appalachia, where I wanted to collect oral histories of mountain women. I could swagger anywhere on The Zack, on Vitamin P. Never mind that even before I'd ever come down with OCD I'd been the anxious, tentative sort. Never mind that unnamed trepidations, for all of my life, had prevented me from taking a trip to New Hampshire for more than a few days. Now that I'd taken the cure, I really could go anywhere, even off to the rippling blue mountains of poverty, far from a phone or a friend.

A gun hung over the door. In the oven I saw a roasted bird covered with flies. In the bathroom, a fat girl stooped over herself without bothering to shut the door, and pulled a red rag from between her legs.

Her name was Kim, her sister's name was Bridget, and their mother and father were Kat and Lonny. All the females were huge and doughy while Lonny stood, a single strand of muscle tanned to the color of tobacco. He said very little while the mother and daughters chattered on, offering me Cokes and Cheerios, showing me to my room where I sat on a lumpy mattress and stared at the white walls.

And then a moon rose. A storm of hurricane force ploughed through fields and sky. I didn't feel myself here. The sound of the storm, battering just above my head, seemed far, far away. There was a whispering in my mind, a noise like silk being split. Next to me, on the night table, my sturdy bottle of Prozac. I was fine. So long as I had that, I would be fine.

I pretended I was fine for the next couple of days, racing around with manic intensity. I sat heavy Kat in one of her oversized chairs and insisted she tell me everything about her life in the Blue Ridge Mountains, scribbling madly as she talked. *I am happy happy happy* I sang to myself. I tried to ignore the strange sounds building in my brain, kindling that crackles, a flame getting hot.

And then I was taking a break out in the sandy yard. It was near one hundred degrees. The sun was tiny in a bleary sky. Chickens screamed and pecked.

In one swift and seamless move, Lonny reached down to grab a bird. His fist closed in on its throat while all the crows cawed and the beasts in my bones brayed away. He laid the chicken down on a stump, raised an ax, and cut. The body did its dance. I watched the severing, how swiftly connections melt, how deep and black is space. Blood spilled.

I ran inside. I was far from a phone or a friend. Maybe I was reminded of some pre-verbal terror: the surgeon's knife, the violet umbilical cord. Or maybe the mountain altitudes had thrown my chemistry off. I don't really know why, or how. But as though I'd never swallowed a Prozac pill, my mind seized and clamped and the obsessions were back.

I took a step forward and then said to myself *don't take another step until you count to twenty-five*. After I'd satisfied that imperative, I had to count to twenty-five again, and then halve twenty-five, and then quarter it, before I felt safe enough to walk out the door. By the end of the day, each step took over ten minutes to complete. I stopped taking steps. I sat on my bed.

"What's wrong with you?" Kat said. "Come out here and talk with us."

I tried, but I got stuck in the doorway. There was a point above the doorway I just had to see, and then see again, and inside of me something screamed *back again back again* and the grief was very large.

For I had experienced the world free and taken in colors and tasted grilled fish and moon. I had left one illness like a too tight snakeskin, and here I was, thrust back. What's worse than illness is to think you're cured—partake of cure in almost complete belief—and then with no warning to be dashed on a dock, moored.

Here's what they don't tell you about Prozac. The drug, for many obsessives who take it, is known to have wonderfully powerful effects in the first few months when it's new to the body. When I called the Prozac Doctor from Kentucky that evening, he explained to me how the drug, when used to treat OCD as opposed to depression, "peaks" at about six months, and then loses some of its oomph. "Someday we'll develop a more robust pill," Dr. Vuckovic said. "In the meantime, up your dose."

I upped my dose. No relief. Why not? Please. Over the months I had come to need Prozac in a complicated way, had come to see it as my savior, half hating it, half loving it. I unscrewed the capsules and poured their contents over my fingers. Healing talc, gone. Dead sand. I fingered the empty husks.

"You'll feel better if you come to church with us," Kat said to me that Sunday morning. She peered into my face, which must have been white and drawn. "Are you suffering from some city sickness?"

I shrugged. My eyes hurt from crying. I couldn't read or write; I could only add, subtract, divide, divide again.

"Come to church," Kat said. "We can ask the preacher to pray for you."

But I didn't believe in prayers where my illness was concerned. I had come to think, through my reading and the words of doctors, and especially through my brain's rapid response to a drug, that whatever was wrong with me had a simplistic chemical cause. Such a belief can be devastating to sick people, for on top of their illness they must struggle with the sense that illness lacks any creative possibilities.

I think these beliefs, so common in today's high tech biomedical era where the focus is relentlessly reductionistic, rob illness of its potential dignity. Illness can be dignified; we can conceive of pain as a kind of complex answer from an elegant system, an arrow pointing inward, a message from soil or sky.

Not so for me. I wouldn't go to church or temple. I wouldn't talk or ask or wonder, for these are distinctly human activities and I'd come to view myself as less than human.

An anger rose up in me then, a rage. I woke late one night, hands fisted. It took me an hour to get out of bed, so many numbers I had to do, but I was determined.

And then I was walking, outside, pushing past the need to count before every step. The night air was muggy, and insects raised a chorus.

I passed midnight fields, a single shack with lighted windows. Cows slept in a pasture.

I rounded the pasture, walked up a hill. And then, before me, spreading out in moonglow, a lake. I stood by its lip. My mind was buzzing and jerking. I don't know at what point the swans appeared—white swans, they must have been, but in silhouette they looked black—that seemed to materialize straight out of the slumbering water. They rose to the surface of the water as memories rise to the surface of consciousness. Hundreds of black swans suddenly, floating absolutely silent, and as I stood there the counting ceased, my mind became silent, and I watched. The swans drifted until it seemed, for a few moments, that they were inside of me, seven dark, silent birds, fourteen princesses, a single self swimming in a tepid sea.

I don't know how long I stood there, or when, exactly, I left. The swans disappeared eventually. The counting ticking talking of my mind resumed.

Still, even in chattering illness, I had been quieted for a bit; doors in me had opened; elegance had entered.

This thought calmed me. I was not completely claimed by illness, nor a prisoner of Prozac, entirely dependent on the medication to function. Part of me was still free, a private space not absolutely permeated by pain. A space I could learn to cultivate.

Over the next few days, I noticed that even in the thicket of obsessions my mind sometimes swam into the world, if only for brief forays. There, while I struggled to take a step, was the sun on a green plate. *Remember that* I said to myself. And here, while I stood fixated in a doorway, was a beetle with a purplish shell like eggplants growing in wet soil. *Appreciate this* I told myself, and I can say I did, those slivers of seconds when I returned to the world. I loved the beetle, ached for the eggplant, paddled in a lake with black swans.

And so a part of me began to learn about living outside the disease, cultivating appreciation for a few free moments. It was nothing I would have wished for myself, nothing to noisily celebrate. But it was something, and I could choose it, even while mourning the paralyzed parts of me, the pill that had failed me.

A long time ago, Freud coined the term "superego." A direct translation from German means "over I." Maybe what Freud meant, or should have meant, was not a punitive voice but the angel in the self who rises above an ego under siege, or a medicated mind, to experience the world from a narrow but occasionally gratifying ledge.

I am thirty-one now, and I know that ledge well. It is a smaller space than I would have wished for myself—I who would like to possess a mind free and flexible. I don't. Even after I raised my dose, the Prozac never worked as well as it once had, and years later I am sometimes sad about that, other times strangely relieved, even though my brain is hounded. I must check my keys, the stove; I must pause many times while I write this and do a ritual count to thirty. It's distracting, to say the least, but still I write this. I can walk and talk and play. I've come to live my life in those brief stretches of silence that arrive throughout the day, working at what I know is an admirable speed, accomplishing all I can in clear pauses, knowing those pauses may be short-lived.

I can in clear pauses, knowing those pauses may be short-lived. I am learning something about the single moment, how rife with potential it is, how truly loud its tick. I have heard clocks and clocks. Time shines, sad and good.

And what of the unclear, mind-cluttered stretches? These, as well, I have bent to. I read books now, even when my brain has real difficulties taking in words. Half a word, or a word blurred by static, is better than nothing at all. There is also a kind of stance I've developed, detaching my mind from my mind, letting the static sizzle on while I walk, talk, read, while the obsessive cycles continue and I, stepping aside, try to link my life to something else. It is a meditative exercise of a high order, and one I'm getting better at. Compensations can be gritty gifts.

Is this adaptation a spiritual thing? When I'm living in moments of clarity, have I transcended disease or has disease transformed me, taught me how to live in secret niches? I don't know.

A few nights ago, a man at a party, a Christian psychologist, talked about the brain. "The amazing thing," he said, "is that if you cut the corpus callosum of small children, they learn without the aid of medication or reparative surgery how to transfer information from the left to the right hemisphere. And because we know cerebral neurons never rejuvenate, that's evidence," he said, "for a mind that lives beyond the brain, a mind outside of our biologies."

Perhaps. Or perhaps our biologies are broader than we ever thought. Perhaps the brain, because of its wound, has been forced into some kink of creativity we can neither see nor explain. This is what the doctors didn't tell me about illness; that an answer to illness is not necessarily cure, but an ambivalent compensation. Disease, for sure, is disorganization, but cure is not necessarily the synthetic pill-swallowing righting of the mess. To believe this is to rigidly define brain function in terms of "normal" and "abnormal," a devastating definition for many. And to believe this, especially where the psyche is concerned, may also mean dependence on psychotropic drugs, and the risk of grave disappointment if the drugs stop working.

I think of those children, their heads on white sheets, their corpus callosums exposed and cut. I wonder who did that to them, and why. I'm sure there is some compelling medical explanation— wracking seizures that need to be stopped—but still, the image disturbs me. I think more, though, of the children's brains once sewn back inside the bony pockets of skull. There, in the secret dark, between wrenched hemispheres, I imagine tiny tendrils growing, between wrenched hemispheres, I imagine tiny tendrils growing, so small and so deep not even the strongest machines can see them. They are real but not real, biological but spiritual. They wind in and out, joining left to right, building webbed wings and rickety bridges, sending out messengers with critical information, like the earliest angels who descended from the sky with news and challenge, wrestling with us in nighttime deserts, straining our thighs, stretching our bodies in pain, no doubt, until our skin took on new shapes.

Lauren Slater won last year Editors' Prize contest for her essay, "Welcome to My Country," part of a memoir of the same title published in February by Random House.

"GEE, IT WAS JUST MEANT TO BE A LITTLE CONSTRUCTIVE CRITICISM."

ROWER AMONG TREES / *Julia Wendell*

Taking out the garbage
again, I came upon a barn owl
resting on a boxwood,
sizing me up as if I, not he,
were the intruder,
emerging from my house
into a chilled gray light,
into the long,
slow first movement
of a daybreak of rain. The cardinal
knew, the cardinal
and the jay and the crow
that this was not my home.
And I thought—
he should have been sleeping
in the hull of his tree by now,
shouldn't he?

He sat unmoved
as I rattled down the drive,
my tin third leg
dragging behind, and was there
when I returned, hinged lids
blinking at me, while I
blinked back.
I smacked my dirty hands together,
wiped them on my dirty jeans,
tuning up for my mistake,
"How-dee-dow, Mr. Owl,"
I called out as he
spread and lifted,
turning up the yellow & red & brown
leaves of maples & pin oaks
as he passed,
as if they were oars lifting
for the next stroke, and he
a tireless rower among trees.

LEARNING TO BREATHE / *Julia Wendell*

1.
After the argument,
after he goes outside with a shovel,
levels the Monet garden,
levels the peach tree
he's taken years to grow, cracks
the orchid bench he
built last year,
after he's done a fair amount
of shouting to the cornfield across the way,
until he no longer has the breath for it,
comes inside, then goes back out again
because he is afraid,
afraid to be too near my accusations—
after the children run out wild-eyed,
and I take them in my arms again,
telling them that we'll work it out
again, though each new time, I never know
if now is the moment that will break
everything, all sirens & red lights & gurneys
& no going back, the way my uncle,
suddenly dead at 62, looked
in his coffin so perfectly resolved
to my mother's final comment: "He dreaded
growing old, and now he never will. . . ."
After all this, I go in, sometime deep
in the late-night reprieve,

2.
I go into my son's room
to watch him sleep.
No cracks showing, so effortless each breath,
and I want only this,
for him to take the next one and the next,
worrying that he'll
always need a little prompting.
When he was born,

he was born "sleepy," swirling along with me
in my Demerol dream.
He didn't almost die, and yet
red lights flashing, white cloaks summoned
huddled round the bassinet
so I wouldn't see the needle
being stabbed into his heart, forcing
him to breathe.
I can't take back the words I've said,
things he's seen, breaths taken,
and to be honest, I wouldn't
even want to. So when I note
the frayed stuffed lop-ear
he's held tight for his 10 years,
now propped above his sleeping head,
still wide-awake, like me, keeping sentry
in the moonlight,

when I see him there like that,
I smell perfume, and a woman's
body, soft arms, soft lips
and a breast that will one day cushion
his ascending and descending breaths.

And then I turn and leave the room.

When I think of god, I think of you
drawing my head into your lap,
knowing I would do most anything
for the blessing of your fingers
moving in my hair, coaxing me farther
& farther into you.

And I think of
clusters of tart grapes bending their vines,
the forest-green nocturne
and decrescendo of the leaves,
the constant, invisible ticking
of the crickets—summer's lullaby.
End of August, and my calendar turns
on its back.

On my birthdays, even as a child
I felt a thickness in the throat
when the hydrangeas were fullest,
when the horses, tails swishing,
waited at the barn door in good faith,
wanting out of the heat, when everything was
a little dusty, a little full,
a cup brimming with the first taste of passing.

Now, as I walk out to our abundant garden
breaking through the webs that thread
our yard, the colors deepen—
it's what I have to lose,
not what I've not yet had
that matters. And the grace
rooted in our garden soil & air
is what wheels above the bedroom nights
when faith & love are not enough,
when the dark perfume of your genitals is.
In your absence,

I cull the twisted stalks of wind-bent gladiolas that
   remain,
collect the softest plum tomatoes that have
fallen through the wire mesh to the ground,
consider the zucchini growing in time lapse
from fingers to clubs.
Forgive me, but I cannot swallow fast enough.
My hair now glistens
with the first few strands of grey,
the skin around my eyes crinkles
like the paper husks of tomatillos.
And drawing your head into the vestibule
of my lap, I hold on,
knowing how fast we grow
to be filled,
to ripen past ripeness, to fall.

BETTER HALF / *Julia Wendell*

"I believe in all sincerity that if each man were not able to
live a number of lives besides his own he would not be
able to live his own life."

—Paul Valéry

Day after ordinary day
I remember what I must conceal,
choosing anybody's life: wife, mother,
suburb, commute,
fluorescent aisles of
Wisk or All, Cheerios or Trix.
I even go to church some Sundays
to sit among the balding, hats, & perms
of the penitent.
I do not want responsibility
for my children's souls.

Yet at night,
when I lay myself down,
the thing starts tapping at my chest—
what exists because of love,
yet has so little to do with love.
What resembles a child's thin arm
or a wand, or a watch,
or a tree sprouting wings.
Anything, really, that I want.

Tonight it eats the food
I have prepared for myself. I have cut
the mango into bite-sized
pieces, sweeter
than clover, more succulent
than water to my parched mouth.

Then it is the man who is you
in among the peppers & zucchinis,
the potatoes & tomatillos,
working his garden.

A woman pulls up in her Maz.
Stepping from the treasure chest
of that small car,
poised, heeled, purring & unperplexed,
she will offer him anything.
Pulling a mauve sweater over her head,
her breasts are full,
nipples dark & erect,
a curtain of light hair falls over them so softly.
She will offer him most anything
with her willingness to undo,
button by button,
the bright artful eradicating surge
of passion. And though
she is no one I know,
when she takes your gardener's cock
in her long hands with the
fire-engine nails,
I must confess, I want her too.
I want her because she is not me.
I want you to want her
because she is not me.

In the morning mirror
I see your eyes staring back,
I feel your hands callused
from making the earth so rich
and fruitful. I feel your hands
on my breasts, which are hers,
as I vanish into the necessary otherness,
the mystery of the passion of not-me.
And suddenly it's at the breakfast table
beside the bagels & jam—
danger rising up
when what I fear most is what I most desire.
This is the jacket of feeling
that binds me: if you love the other too hard,
I can't stand it.
If you don't love her hard enough...
Well then, I wouldn't have any of this,
would I?

VISITOR / *Julia Wendell*

All morning the moon
hung bright & full
over my new 83 acres,
refusing to say
'So long'—night's shoulder
tattoo, butterfly, rose, metaphor
for survival.
Or did it only
want to be the sun?
I don't know
what makes the world
so full of wonder,
why this moonlit morning was unlike
any other, or even why
you pointed it out to me now,
as you once had most everything
worth noting—beetles, moles, stars—the years
we were together. So close
to understanding
that you became that round thing
stuck in its sky,
as well as the geldings grazing
under it, a little miffed
and not yet ready to come out
from under their blanket
of night—even became
the woman who woke you
before you were ready,
as she slipped beside
you, in friendship,
feeling for your hand
as if it were her own,
spooning you awake.
Though her smells had moved
from Opium
to horses, Salems,
& another man's sweat,

she was still shaped the same,
permanent as a favorite song
stuck in your head,
or a moon that won't
come down from its ladder.
Love is stubborn
like that, a ghost
stalling day's engine,
a carpenter after hours
who works by touch, sculpting
shadows, guided by the edge
of the last rung,
or how a certain wood
feels, the old shapes
that take new shape in the dark.

Julia Wendell's third collection of poems, *Wheeler Lane*, will be published in 1996.

WHY RICHARD CAN'T / *Nanci Kincaid*

T HERE WERE ENDLESS GOOD reasons. For months now, Richard had lain in bed running over the list in his head, adding to it as though the reasons were dollars and he was wisely depositing them in a savings account.

First of all, Mona was twelve years younger than he was. This is where he began each night. He lay on his back, legs spread, hands folded behind his head, staring at the ceiling fan. The woman is thirty-six years old he thought. In the dark she looks younger. When Richard was sixty-one Mona would still be in her forties. He shuddered.

Granted, there was something to be said for younger women, the way coeds bolted across campus with a mix of hurriedness and forever in their gait. Something to be said for firm breasts and shiny hair and mouths that had not said everything already or been kissed enough for the thrill to be gone from it. Richard noticed these things. He wasn't dead. He was sensible. He didn't want to attach himself to some younger woman who would remind him constantly that he was aging. "Good lord, Richard," Mona said, "I'm thirty-six years old. Nobody can accuse you of robbing the cradle."

Sometimes Mona wasn't sensitive to the point he was making.

Number two: Mona had children. Richard had never had children of his own and the truth was they scared him. He didn't know how to talk to them. He couldn't tell what they were thinking. And Mona's children were girls. Two teenage girls. My God, he must be crazy. What would it be like to live in a house full of Tampax and telephone calls, and barelegged females walking around in toenail polish and T-shirts? He supposed there must be a great deal of crying in a house full of women, and giggling too. He feared he might become the source of their private jokes and not know it, that laughter would gush from Mona and her daughters like a kind of sympathy.

Oh, the reasons were endless. It made no sense to dwell on it night after night. WHY I CAN'T MARRY MONA. *She is not my type, really. She expects things from me that I almost certainly cannot deliver. She thinks I am a better man than I am. Her divorce has made a mess of her—she doesn't know her own head yet. She couldn't possibly marry me until she finds herself.* That sounded right, didn't it? Did women still 'find themselves' in the nineties? Did they still lose themselves in the men they married? Richard didn't know. He knew Mona looked at him with more sting than any woman ever had.

Mona had been in his graduate American Literature class for almost six weeks when it occurred to Richard, much to his horror, that he loved her. She sat in the back, listening, amused. He measured the success of his lectures against her response to them. He couldn't seem to make her understand the magnificence of artistic suffering. A great artist must suffer, he told her, but he couldn't make her feel it. She said *Moby Dick* was boring. Boring. She said it was a man's story and didn't particularly interest her. Chasing a whale is a small thing, she said, compared with raising children. Chasing a whale is a luxury. Richard had never heard anything so ignorant in his whole life. She had gone on to say that Thoreau was self-reverent, not self-reliant. She said a life separate from other lives, untangled, unanchored, uncommitted is the life of a coward.

"Who couldn't have a lofty thought or two with all that leisure time on his hands?" she asked. "Who did Thoreau ever look out for other than himself? If he'd raised children on Walden Pond, fed them, clothed them, educated them, while thinking his thoughts, then that would be something. Of course, if he'd had children to raise he wouldn't have had time to think so much...unless, of course, he'd had a wife...."

"What kind of convoluted reason is that?" Richard had practically shouted at Mona. "There is more to life than raising children, Ms. Montgomery."

"Particularly if you don't have any," she said in a voice that embarrassed him, making him feel limited—and furious.

Mona had gone on to write a long paper on why Mark Twain was a sexy writer and Melville was an intellectual one. She said intelligence was sexy, but intellectualism was not. The woman didn't know what the hell she was talking about. But the younger students, particularly the male students, stared at her when she spoke in class. They radiated a peculiar affection for Mona which Richard found disturbing. Mona was too old for the young men in American Lit. What did they know about pleasing a woman with two teenage daughters and absurd literary opinions? Mona had wisps of grey in her hair, he hoped they noticed that. She was out of style, dated; yet he heard girls invite her to lunch after class and young men offer to buy her a beer. And before he knew what he was doing, in a stupid moment after one particularly painful class, Richard asked Mona to go for coffee. It seemed important to him that she understand. "*Moby Dick* is the greatest book ever written," Richard insisted, "with the possible exception of the *Bible*. The power of his vision...."

"It's a small, limited vision," Mona replied. "A man who doesn't know anything at all about women just isn't very interesting, Richard. I'm sorry."

Richard was stupefied by her certainty. He couldn't decide whether to be angry or amused.

Mona smiled. "And he's godawful boring, Richard."

Why did everything she said feel like a personal attack on him? When Mona spoke of Melville did she really mean Richard? He thought she did. He would show her he wasn't boring. Maybe she thought she had nothing to learn from him, but he would teach her a thing or two.

They walked to a coffee shop near campus where Mona told him about an affair she had had—the only affair of her life—with the golf pro at Brook Valley Country Club, which had made her realize how desperately she needed to divorce her husband. She said she cried for a year. She very nearly cried telling the story. Richard was terrified by her honesty. It seemed so reckless—telling the truth. "Should you be telling me this?" Richard asked. "You hardly know me. For all you know I might...."

"Blackmail me?" Mona said, taking a bite of chicken salad. Richard couldn't take his eyes off her. He didn't dare mention Herman Melville again for fear of breaking the spell. Besides, he was too nervous. He had been nervous since he first laid eyes on Mona. But he had been even more nervous when she invited him to eat supper with her daughters and her. She made chili dogs with onions and poured potato chips into a bowl and served baked beans crusted with brown sugar.

"This is Dr. Petreman," Mona had said when Richard arrived at the door carrying an eighteen-dollar bottle of wine and feeling like a carry-over from some earlier civilization, "my English professor. I've told you about him."

Her daughters smiled, looking him over carefully. He felt like a foreigner who didn't understand the language. Mona's daughters asked him questions. He did his best to answer them. Yes, the fraternity parties are said to be wild. Yes, he supposed there were lots of cute guys at the University. No, he had missed the Pro-

Choice march. No, he did not attend the 'Take Back the Night' rally. Suddenly he wanted to apologize for that.

He looked at Mona's two slender, dark-eyed daughters, both of them with curly hair like their mother, the youngest one wearing braces, the oldest one wearing earrings made of feathers. They were lovely girls, he thought. But what could they expect from life? Their knowledge of world issues came largely from television. They couldn't believe Richard had never watched a single hour of *Oprah Winfrey*. "You're kidding?" they kept saying. "You don't know what you're missing." That was exactly the feeling Richard had when he left Mona's house that night to go home.

Love is not reason enough to marry someone. Richard knew this. *Great sex is not reason enough either.* Even together the two are not enough. Mona had reduced Richard to a teenager. He had erections talking to her on the phone. She could not stop by his office without his wanting to kiss her and unbutton her blouse. The first time they made love he had nearly cried from the intensity of it. It was as though Mona had dismantled him, loved him in fragments, then reassembled him into an entirely new man.

When she clung to him in the darkness, saying his name over and over, climbing him and then flying from him, falling, floating, moaning, he held her as though she were his own life come loose from him. He tried to press himself through her skin and make himself a permanent place inside her. He had gone crazy, he was sure. But the only time he clearly recognized his own existence and believed there was good reason for it was when Mona called his name. "Richard," she whispered. "Richard, Richard, Richard. . . . "

There were so many good reasons why he couldn't marry Mona. *For one thing he was not absolutely sure Mona wanted to marry him.* She had never said so. Sometimes she said, "If we lived together, Richard, we could rent black-and-white movies and watch them in our pajamas. We could have dinner parties and invite only the people we like best. We could make love in every room of the house. . . . " But Mona never said, "If we were married. . . . "

It wasn't that women were some entirely new experience for him. Richard was a handsome man who had been told so often enough. He ran three miles a day and ate sensibly. He noticed women notice. He had even had involvements, but none of them had seemed worth reconstructing his life to accommodate. He had decided at one point, nearly ten years ago, to stop noticing women entirely, except in intellectual and professional circumstances. And, to tell the truth, it hadn't been that hard to do. In that time he had published three scholarly books and countless critical articles. His life was well organized and under control.

Then came Mona with her curly brown hair, little wisps of grey in it, her stinging eyes, and her crinkles of crows' feet that Richard found strangely sexy. She sat in the back of his class by the window. When she smiled her face was full of line and curve. When Richard said something that Mona found particularly absurd, she squinted at him the way a mother gazes at a child who has misunderstood something important. There was tolerance in her expression. She was so unimpressed with logic that he found her totally unnerving.

"The next year I was a Rhodes scholar," Richard explained. "I studied at Oxford."

"Oh," Mona said, smiling. "I was at Oxford too. I was Ole Miss homecoming queen my sophomore year."

For one fleeting moment it had seemed to Richard that her accomplishment far exceeded his own. It seemed impossible to impress a woman who had once worn a crown and been paraded through town on an elaborate float made of pink toilet paper. He pictured Mona smiling and waving to admiring subjects who lined the streets for miles.

He would like to have believed Mona was stupid and small-minded, to dismiss her on the grounds that she was uninsightful and under-read, but instead he began to question his own world-view. How many good movies had he missed?

While Richard was reading Kant and Camus and wrestling with deconstruction, Mona had been reading fairy tales to her children. She had lived a life in which Santa Claus, the Tooth Fairy, and the Easter Bunny had all figured significantly. They were no more absurd to her than Picasso, Matisse, Faulkner. In fact, it seemed to Richard that because Mona could conduct her life as though there really were a white rabbit that delivered colored eggs on Easter morning, she could also look at Picasso's cubist women and see herself as clearly as if looking in a mirror. She looked at Matisse's voluptuous reclining women, their rooms full of color and pattern, their legs open, their heads thrown back, as if looking at photos of her sorority sisters in a college yearbook. Mona had never been to London, Rome or Paris, but Richard had never been to Disney World or Yellowstone or the Grand Ole Opry.

Every morning he ordered himself to stop thinking about marrying Mona, to stop imagining what their life together might be like. And every night he began counting again. One night he had counted up thirty-four very convincing reasons WHY I CANNOT MARRY MONA. He lay in bed with tears in his eyes thinking of the reasons, particularly reason number thirty-four, a reason that twisted like a knife in his belly. Richard could not marry Mona because—oh, it was a hateful fact, the undoing of which would be no less agonizing than undoing his birth to a particular pair of parents, or undoing his age, or the color of his eyes. Richard could not marry Mona because he was already married.

Richard turned to look at the woman beside him in bed. Joanna was asleep, her mouth open slightly, her short grey hair in place. It amazed Richard the way Joanna slept so neatly that when she awoke in the morning her hair was unmussed. She could get dressed and go off to her job at the bank without combing it at all if she wished. He had learned to admire her absence of vanity, the fact that she did not color her hair to hide the grey the way so many women her age did, the fact that she wore her hair in an efficient haircut. She was the most sensible woman he had ever encountered, and he had admired that about her almost from the beginning. She had expected very little of him during their twenty-seven-year marriage, because she understood, Richard believed, the importance of his academic work, the fact that he had needed large amounts of time alone, undistracted by the details of everyday life. She had never allowed domesticity to suck energy from his intellectual life. No children. No pets. No wife in an apron anxiously waiting for him to come home. For much of their married life Joanna had earned the larger income. She had always managed their money and made their investment decisions and deserved full credit for the fact that at this point in their lives they were financially secure—even prosperous.

Over the years Richard and Joanna had developed an understanding. She had overlooked his few indiscretions that had come to her attention. Their second year of marriage he had forgiven her for cutting her nearly waist-length hair—which she had always worn parted in the middle and hanging straight down her back. Often while sitting in the sun to let it dry, she would brush the tangles from it and it would fly from her head full of electricity. Then one Friday afternoon Richard came home and found Joanna standing in the kitchen, pleased, not more than three inches of hair anywhere on her head. "What do you think?" she said.

This was the first of many opportunities Richard had missed to tell Joanna what he really thought. "Why did you do it?" he asked.

She smiled and hugged him. "You are looking at the new assistant corporate loan officer of People's National Bank!" The following morning she went to work wearing a new grey wool suit—the sparkle in her eyes having focused. Years later Richard had had to forgive her, happily, for being a greater financial success than he was. His academic books had not sold particularly well, although one had been very generously reviewed in the *New York Times*. Joanna knew most of the worst things about Richard's personality as he did about hers, and those worst things had been accepted. So what if they never laughed together. Marriage wasn't a laughing matter, was it?

"Mona," Richard explained. "I have been married to the same woman for twenty-seven years. How many men do you know who can say that?"

She looked at him with her squinting eyes and said, "Yes, Richard, but are you happy? Do you love your wife?"

As she so often did, Mona had missed the point entirely. Richard found her exasperating. She had divorced her husband because, "We weren't happy anymore and lost our hope of ever being happy together again." When Richard asked Mona for a further explanation she touched his face softly, and shook her head. "Life is short, Richard," she said.

More than once Richard decided never to see Mona again. More than once he announced his intention to her. "Mona, there are too many reasons why this will never work. I've been a married man more than half my life. My father was married sixty-three years. Marriage runs in my family, Mona. Petreman men get married for life."

Mona smiled at Richard as though he were saying exactly the opposite of what he was actually saying. "Do you know what I hope?" Mona said. "I hope that when you get to heaven God will be well pleased. I hope he will give you a blue ribbon and let you wear it all through eternity. He will say over the loudspeaker of heaven, 'Honor this man. He lived all of his life with a woman he didn't love. He resisted happiness when it presented itself. He lived his life as though it were a punishment. Give this man a pair of wings. He is a saint! He is....'"

Before Mona finished speaking Richard pulled her to him and began kissing her angrily. "Damn you, Mona," he whispered. He locked the door and made love to Mona in his office in the English building. The world of academia traveled the halls outside, students coming and going, professors thinking, the cleaning lady sweeping. Afterward he held her, her wild, curly hair a mess, her body bearing a history that seemed to him, at the moment, more important than the history of the civilized world. He ached over the fact that she had lived thirty-six basically satisfactory years without him. They lay on the floor of his carpeted office. Twice she pulled away from him to stand up and get dressed. Both times he refused to let her go. "Stay a little longer," he whispered, "please."

That night he called her and said, "Mona, this is Richard." His voice was formal and businesslike. "I am calling to let you know that I cannot possibly continue to see you. I hope you will understand and forgive me."

"I'm sure that is a very wise decision," Mona said after a moment of silence.

A week later Richard invited Mona to travel with him to a literary conference in St. Louis where he was presenting a paper titled "Thoreau: Self-Reliance or Self-Reverence?" Mona read the title and was very moved. She said yes, she would love to spend a week with him in St. Louis.

What she didn't know was that Richard had decided to tell her once and for all that their relationship must end. He had never wanted less to do anything in his life, but he had to do it or go mad. He couldn't spend another year ignoring his academic work and thinking up ways to spend time with Mona. He had become a spectacular liar in the last year. And poor Joanna accepted anything Richard said without question. He must put a stop to the lying. Regain control. Get back on track.

But how do you tell the woman you love that you have decided not to love her? The pleasures of the trip, he hoped, would help soften the blow. He wouldn't break the news to Mona until the very last day. Until then, they could just continue to love each other and be happy.

Mona made arrangements for her daughters to stay with their

father and bought a wonderful black dinner dress, two silk blouses, and a nightgown the color of peach sherbet, all of which she showed Richard, stopping by his office, flushed with excitement, on her way home from the mall. This had touched Richard deeply. He knew that Mona could not afford such purchases.

Richard spent most of the day before the trip shopping for and packing a picnic in a Styrofoam cooler. He made chicken sandwiches. He bought wine. He bought chocolate chip cookies, and fruit, and crackers and cheese and French bread from the bakery. He remembered the corkscrew. He brought cloth napkins— a detail that surprised and pleased him. He packed carefully, including vast numbers of maps and his favorite tapes. He whistled as he loaded the car.

Determined not to spoil the trip by dwelling on the inevitable nature of his mission, Richard put telling Mona good-bye almost completely out of his mind. He felt, instead, as if it were Joanna to whom he was saying good-bye forever.

Richard held Mona's hand as they drove past the city limits sign. Then he said the most foolish thing he had ever said in his life. He said, "Mona, let's pretend we just got married and we're going to St. Louis on our honeymoon. Let's pretend we've got forever stretched out in front of us."

Mona squeezed his hand and looked at him, her face radiating a mixture of desire and suspicion. "Richard," she said smiling, "I've been pretending that all along."

They picnicked at roadside parks, fed each other bites of cheese and cracker, and kissed like lovesick teenagers. In the car they listened to Chopin until Mona fell asleep, her head resting on Richard's shoulder. Afterwards he found a country music channel and the hopelessly sentimental lyrics revived Mona. She knew the words to every song and sang out loud. Richard even found himself quite taken by a line in one song, 'I sleep without you, but I dream about you.' "That's beautiful," he said.

Mona told Richard stories about her children. How her youngest daughter had asked for a different pet every year, a dog, a cat, a goldfish, a hamster, a rabbit, and finally, a boa constrictor. Mona had drawn the line there. Mona saw sexual symbolism everywhere she turned, which, she explained to Richard, had to do with being a woman and having a body flooded with estrogen.

Richard laughed at the boa constrictor story. He laughed at the tale of Mona's older sister telling her that men's penises were the same size as their feet, and Mona believing it. She and her fifth-grade girlfriends had taken up asking boys what size shoe they wore—and had received the boys' hesitant answers with curiosity and horror.

But the most amazing thing was that Richard found himself pouring out the stories of his life—letting Mona taste them, drink them, digest them. And—dammit—it didn't hurt to do it. For the first time in his life, maybe, he wanted to talk. He even told Mona about his mother. What the hell was happening?

In St. Louis Richard delivered his paper. He attended the reading of two papers where he felt obligated to make an appearance. Otherwise he hardly left the hotel room. The room was air-conditioned and the curtains drawn, simulating endless night. Richard and Mona spent days in bed, talking, laughing, making love as though sex were something terribly expensive that they had never been able to afford—until now. They ordered room service nine straight meals.

Only one night during the week did they go out for dinner, and that was so Mona's new black dress wouldn't be wasted. She bathed and put hot curlers in her hair—which startled Richard—and made up her eyes and put on perfume. With equal parts of alarm and amazement Richard watched Mona assemble herself. In the end he thought her cosmetics had done little to damage the natural blush she had taken on during the week.

It was not until the first night of this trip that Richard had ever seen Mona with no make-up at all, fresh, wet, right out of the shower, wrapped in a faded cotton robe. Mona had been shy coming out of the bathroom. Richard lay on the bed watching the news. He stood up when Mona entered.

"Don't stare at me," she said.

"I can't help it," Richard stammered. "You look so..."

"Wet?"

"Wonderful." Richard knew how stupid he sounded. He knew Mona didn't believe him for a minute. "Let me look at you."

He wanted to say that she was beautiful, because that's what a man should say, that's what a woman expects to hear. But the truth was he had no idea whether or not Mona was beautiful at this moment. He doubted it. She looked too small, like she had showered away all the adult and was standing barefooted before him, as a little girl, totally uncamouflaged. He was overcome with the desire to protect her. To throw her to the ground and wrap himself around her while fighter planes flew overhead dropping bombs all around them.

Nervously, Mona untied the sash of her bathrobe and let it fall open, not like a woman being sexy, but like a woman being brave. Her imperfect breasts, her full hips, the Caesarean scar that ran down her tummy. She was all curve, and softness and strength. Her body was beautiful *because* it was battle-scarred, Richard thought. He wanted to tell her so, but couldn't. He stepped toward her, slid his hands inside her robe, and buried his face in the dampness of her neck. "Mona," he said. "You scare the hell out of me."

"That's not a very nice thing to say to a naked woman," Mona whispered.

Richard lifted her in his arms and carried her to the bed. "I feel like I'm in some goddamned movie. This is real, isn't it, Mona? This is really happening?"

"It's definitely happening to me," Mona whispered.

Later he sat in the bathroom and watched Mona as she dried her hair and put on make-up. "Why do you put that stuff on your eyes?"

"It's eyeliner. It makes my eyes show up."

"What about that stuff?"

"Mascara? You're kidding." Mona turned to stare at Richard. "Doesn't your wife wear any make-up?"

Richard thought a minute. "I don't know. I don't think so."

"Oh, great."

"What?"

"I find it horrifying to think your wife is so beautiful she wears no make-up at all, Richard. But I find it even more horrifying that in twenty-seven years you haven't looked closely enough to be sure."

"I don't want to talk about Joanna."

"Just one question."

"Oh, god," Richard moaned.

"Do you love her, Richard?"

Richard wanted to say "Yes, damn it, I love my wife!" He wanted to say it for Joanna's sake, who deserved at least that after all this time, and for Mona's sake because he understood that, strangely enough, his loving Joanna would make Mona think better of him. But mostly he wished it for himself. He wished he were capable of sustained love. He wished the structure of his life was based on something more than habit. But the truth was that whatever combination of things he felt for Joanna now, it wasn't love. Mona had shown him that. "I love you, Mona," Richard said, recklessly. "That's all I know."

That night before they went to dinner Richard shaved while Mona watched, like a scene in a television advertisement. He took his time, shaving slowly. He put on his dark suit. Mona had never seen him in it. It was an expensive suit that often caused attractive women to smile at him and ask how tall he was.

Dinner was elegant. Dinner was outrageously expensive. But what did it matter? For Richard the evening had taken on the proportions of the Last Supper. He ordered more wine. He and Mona looked intently into each other's eyes, entire sentences evaporating as they were spoken. Words were reduced to accessories, intimate messages exchanged by code. It seemed to Richard that all around him people were smiling approval.

"How long can this last?" Richard asked Mona as they lay in bed later, tipsy. "How long until these feelings run out? And then what? What comes next?"

"You think we're on the fly-now-pay-later plan, don't you, Richard?" Mona said.

"Are we?" he asked

"I'm not," she said.

Richard rolled over and stared at the ceiling. Everything Mona said came at him like soft bullets, not because what she said was true, but because she thought it was true. That hurt just as much. That she believed he was afraid. She never said so, but sometimes he thought he saw it in her eyes. "I never said I was a hero," Richard said.

"Heroism is not required," Mona said. "You make me happier than I've ever been in my life."

And this was the insanity of it all. Richard heard Mona's words and believed them. He knew it was the truth.

"I never believed this kind of happiness existed," he said, turning to face Mona. "I'm almost fifty years old and happiness scares me, Mona."

Mona rolled up on her elbows and smiled at Richard. "Everybody's afraid of being happy, Richard, that's why they have so many rules against it."

For that one week in St. Louis Richard possessed Mona. He was ashamed to think in those terms. Wasn't that what led many a man to ruin, the insatiable desire to possess a woman? The endless effort to win her, over and over again, to claim her, as one claimed a scientific discovery that would bear his name forever? Men like their names on things—inventions, diseases, bodies of land, bodies of women. Didn't every man want to leave his mark on the woman he loved—a tiny scar on her heart in the shape of his initials? Was Richard any different? Why did he love hearing Mona say his name in the urgent moments of her orgasm? Why did the sound of his own name please him so much?

By the end of the week in St. Louis Richard began to dread the return ride home. He decided to postpone telling Mona good-bye until then. Until they were practically entering the city limits of their other lives. Richard began a silent countdown. Only three more days he told himself. Just two more days. My God, only one day left. Then he counted hours. Twenty-one hours. Twelve hours. Eight hours. He tightened himself into knots as the week came to an end.

On their last day in St. Louis Mona realized that she had not called her daughters all week. And Richard had not called Joanna.

Richard imagined himself sleeping in Joanna's bed when he got home. It suddenly seemed to him to be HER bed. The entire house seemed to be HER house. HER cars. HER furniture. HER bank accounts. HER life in which he rented a small room, a narrow side of the double bed. When had she last known that he was in bed beside her? When had she last cared? Richard could not remember the last time they made love. Why had he stopped kissing her? Why had he stopped watching her undress and lie down next to him? Why had he stopped reaching for her in the darkness? It had all ceased to occur to him years ago. Perhaps because it had ceased to occur to Joanna several years before that. She had not announced it, but it had become perfectly clear. And he had found her indifference satisfactory. A relief. Now when he walked into a room where she was undressing, or when he rolled against her in bed, he said, "Excuse me." But when, exactly, had she started sleeping with her back to him?

During their ride home from St. Louis it rained. The windshield wipers slapped back and forth, but the rain was relentless, and slowed the return trip. Richard sank into a melancholy that Mona's forced cheerfulness could not lift. Five or six times he tried to launch into the exiting lines he had rehearsed so diligently: "I don't know how to tell you this, Mona."

It was stupid and useless. Richard was a coward. If he hadn't been forty-eight years old he might have done something crazy

like fly to Las Vegas and get a quickie divorce and have a quickie
wedding. He might just keep driving and see where they ended
up, Key West maybe, or Mexico. It was too late. It was too late
for everything. How had he wasted so much time?

"Richard," Mona said, "are you okay?"

"No," he said. "And I don't want to talk about it."

When they arrived at Mona's place her ex-husband was there
with the girls. He was pleasant, younger than Richard, athletic
looking. He reached out to shake Richard's hand, but Richard
quickly handed him Mona's suitcase, as if he misunderstood the
gesture. He could not bear to shake hands with any man Mona
had ever loved. Some other man unable to make Mona happy.
The sight of the man made him sick. Richard was rude. He said
good-bye to Mona as though he were a chaperone who had taken
her on an educational field trip.

"Thank you for one of the loveliest weeks of my life," she said.

"You're quite welcome," Richard said in an official, unfamiliar
voice. He sounded like an English professor.

They shook hands in the driveway. He would not let his eyes
meet Mona's for fear they would betray him with sloppy emotion.
She held his hand a few seconds too long so that he had to pull
away from her.

The rain was beginning to clear as Richard drove away. He saw
Mona in his rearview mirror, standing in the driveway, her hair
wild and frizzy from the rain.

"How was St. Louis?" Joanna asked.

"Fine," Richard said.

"That's good." Joanna was putting on her raincoat. "There's left-
over Chinese take-out in the refrigerator if you're hungry."

"I'm not hungry," Richard said.

Joanna picked up the car keys from the kitchen counter and
dropped them in her purse. "I won't be late," she said. "It's
Tuesday, you know." Richard nodded. On Tuesday evenings Joanna
had a directors' meeting at the bank.

"Did you miss me?" Richard said.

Joanna looked at him and offered a dismissive grin. She opened
the closet and began looking for her umbrella.

"Answer me," Richard demanded.

"Richard, what's wrong with you?"

"I want to know if you missed me. I was gone a week, I want to know if you noticed."

"Don't shout at me. I don't know why you're acting this way, but I'm late already...."

"Don't go."

"What?"

"Skip the meeting. Stay home and talk to me."

"Have you gone crazy?"

"It's me or the bank, you choose."

"You've been drinking," Joanna said. "God, Richard, act your age. Go to bed." And before he could answer she walked out of the house and closed the door behind her.

Richard stood at the kitchen window and watched Joanna walk to the car, get in, fasten her seatbelt, and back out onto the street. The sight of her leaving, driving away, disappearing around the corner, gave him an incredible feeling of freedom. Suppose she just kept going? Suppose she never came back? For a minute the world seemed full of possibility. Richard thought of running to the phone to call Mona. "Joanna's gone forever," he would say.

But nothing like that would ever happen. Joanna would come home and he would be there when she did, tonight, and every night afterwards, because, for some reason, they both wanted it that way. They had faced the disappointment that comes if a couple is together long enough—and now there was nothing more to fear.

He didn't want to choose happiness again because he was forty-eight and too tired to work that hard at anything. He would never want to turn Mona into the woman he had turned Joanna into. That's why he stayed married to Joanna, who neither saw him, nor heard him, nor missed him when he was gone. That's why he would always stay. Not because he was afraid of happiness, but because he was afraid of the thing that comes after the happiness.

"I'll tell Mona good-bye tomorrow," Richard said out loud. "I swear to God, I'll tell her first thing tomorrow."

Richard knew that that night he would lie in bed beside Joanna constructing a new, updated list, WHY I CAN'T MARRY MONA. My god, would he spend the rest of his life this way? What kind of man was he? What kind of life was this? He sat at the kitchen table, his face buried in his hands, and thought about Mona. Mona standing in her robe in the hotel room, her wet hair, her nervous smile. "But are you happy, Richard? Do you love your wife?" she had asked him.

Richard ran his finger over the salt and pepper shakers sitting on the kitchen table—he and Joanna had gotten them as a wedding gift, an ordinary set of green shakers with an S painted on one and a P on the other. But over the years the S and the P rubbed off. Now you couldn't tell the salt from the pepper until you shook it out on your plate. Life is so damned sad, Richard thought.

Nanci Kincaid's first novel is *Crossing the Blood*. Another novel, *Balls*, and a collection of stories, *Pretending the Bed was a Raft*, are forthcoming in 1996-7.

"I'M JUST A LAYMAN, BUT I'LL DRINK TO THAT. HERE'S TO THE CREATIVE PROCESS."

AT THE WALL OF FLAME / *Liz Rosenberg*

"Love, that moves the sun, and the other stars."

Here may be suffering, but not death,
promised Virgil—but how would he know?
Always the calm guide, gliding through the waters of
    philosophy,
the good citizen, neither in heaven nor in hell.
Here Virgil stops, a great change comes
at this crossing, when Dante passes through
the flaming wall, like melting glass, in agony, alone
to where his blessed lady waits gaudy in red and gold—
the white-heat of his passion fanned alive for thirty
    years
cool now as the waters of Paradise.
She must have seemed a statue, a stone—
and Virgil, fast-disappearing into oblivion
at the curve of heaven, the beloved guide a ghost
whom no hand touches, and no fire burns.

THE WINDOW / *Liz Rosenberg*

In the window across the street the passersby walk by blurry, in colors of a circus poster, fleeting as clouds. Hear the rattle of cars, see the pink coat passing in the dark glass. If something trembles, is it a fault in the world, a loose pane, or a problem in the cornea? A local woman smears her naked body with chocolate, presents herself to a neighbor as an Easter present— what mania? How many days of false spring, false promise, a neighbor's wave mistaken as an obscene invitation? Consider it from his side; how she passed like a shudder over the lens of his horrified eye. Then you look across at the window again: see a dark square made up of two rectangles, framed in blue paint, with nothing inside.

AT SEVENTEEN / *Liz Rosenberg*

I wanted you all summer while you slept—or tried
to sleep, inching yourself farther from me and closer
   to the wall.
Searching for clues, the slightest sign, I watched all
that hot June while you lay like a child in fever, and
   once you cried
Liz! I can't sleep! so mournfully I almost fled
to the next life where I wouldn't feel so lonely, so cast
   out.
One cat slept on my lap, one on my chest, and God
   knows how
I didn't die of heat prostration. But you'd died. You
   were dead,
you said, your heart had turned to stone.
I stroked your hair back from your forehead,
held your hot hand, and laid my own head on the
   empty space
above your ribs. I spent that summer alone
to keep you company, to prove you weren't dead.
Once, I'd felt your heart pound, felt your arms tremble
   when we kissed.

AT EIGHT A.M. / *Liz Rosenberg*

Like a servant in the old courts of nobility
I walk a discreet three yards behind my son
and his best friend, walking to school, their giant
    backpacks
tails wagging the dog, as if they were going to be
jet-propelled. They're not. They dawdle along the way,
hunkering down sometimes, and bumping into one
    another,
spinning planets on the loose.
Finally their extra-sensory perception tells them a grown-
    up
is lurking around—my bootheels clacking on concrete,
and one of them turns, and then the other, slowly,
    regally.
"I just want to make sure you're safe!" I say,
hunching my shoulders beggar-style. "Look, I'm not
    bothering you."
My son gestures with one hand, like the Pope.
"Come walk with us. We *want* you to."
Now they can go back to full-time daydreaming,
no interruptions at the curb—they glide across,
looking no ways but down, and once I have escorted
    them
inside the school—where the principal stands yelling in
    his big voice
at the steel door, "Slow down! Don't run! Hurry up!"
I walk back down leaf-littered streets, peopled by
    ghosts—
last year's baby-sitter stands waiting for a bus, my
    brother-in-law
safely asleep in Cleveland, lounges on the corner,
    reading the daily news,
back to the great ghost, still sleeping upstairs;
the father of the prince, my husband, old man of the
    castle
ruling the final ruins of his dreams.

HOSPITAL ELEVATOR / *Liz Rosenberg*

With grime-blackened fingernails
he touches her face with the back of his hand
while she makes that long, slow, secretive swipe that
   wipes away tears.
Flat on her back on the hospital gurney, her hair cropped
   short,
the IV swaying beside her like a giant tear.
They fix their eyes together on the elevator buttons,
watching it fall; then, still bending toward her,
he follows her into the open lobby.
Such sadness and worry bends them, they're already
saying goodbye. And how shall we stand it,
how shall we bear it,
what good can come of all this?
I beg you to send them health, Lord;
or if not health then comfort;
and if not even comfort then brandish a radiance
from your broken sparks brilliant enough
to make these sorrows possible to bear.

WHAT ENDURES / *Liz Rosenberg*

The silvery leaves of the dusty miller
shone tough all winter, and the green herb sage
lived off the fat of its own scent,
and one or two drab birds
stayed back to tell us what they meant,
while the white birch shrugged its shoulder and grew
    higher.
Above it all, the sky,
color of wet cement
in January, blue-eyed sweetness in July,
or green as mint
above the sea, the sky was here
above us, on horrific, lean, bare
mornings sparked with fire
pink as a flower
in the hour
before sunset, gun-metal gray, or white
with snow, the old sky peaceful and star-struck all night.

FALL INTO WINTER / *Liz Rosenberg*

Purple as my heart is, evening
glitters the flowers into foil.
The light season passing,
days growing short of breath.
Moonlight, lift up your heavy skirts
and walk with me into the river
where the old winter dreams sink,
where hope is still swimming.

Liz Rosenberg's most recent book of poems is *Children of Paradise*. Her first novel, *Heart and Soul*, will be published this year.

William Maxwell

© Brookie Maxwell

William Maxwell is the author of six novels and five collections of short fiction, most recently *All The Days and Nights: The Collected Stories*, published in 1994. His 1980 novel, *So Long, See You Tomorrow*, won the American Book Award. He is also the author of a family history, *Ancestors*.

Maxwell was born in Lincoln, Illinois where he lived until the age of 14, when his family moved to Chicago. After graduating from the University of Illinois and a brief stint in graduate school, Maxwell went to New York to seek his fortune as a writer. He was hired by *The New Yorker* in 1936, where he spent the next 40 years as a fiction editor and occasional essay reviewer. The writers he edited include J.D. Salinger, John Cheever, John O'Hara, Harold Brodkey, and Delmore Schwartz.

This interview was conducted by Kay Bonetti in November 1995 in New York City for the American Audio Prose Library, which has recordings of readings by and interviews with 131 contemporary writers. For a free catalog of AAPL listings, write PO Box 842, Columbia, MO 65205, or call 800-447-2275. A second part of this interview will appear in the next issue of *The Missouri Review*.

An Interview with
William Maxwell / *Kay Bonetti*

Interviewer: Could we start by getting on the record some of the details of your chronology and your life? You were born in 1908 in Lincoln, Illinois?

Maxwell: Lincoln was a small town of twelve thousand people. My mother's father was a judge. My father's father was a lawyer. Behind them on both sides were country people. My father's father died just as he was beginning to make a career for himself, but my father's youth was rather poverty stricken. So he was always careful about money all his life, and preparing for a rainy day that never came. The pattern of our family life was that he came home on Friday afternoon and left Tuesday morning, and traveled the road with a heavy suitcase full of printed forms, which he used when he was visiting local insurance agents. My mother and father, insofar as I'm able to say, were very much in love with each other. When he came home on Friday afternoons we were always waiting on the front porch—he was embraced with affection when he came home. We lived in a big old house with rooms that were hard to heat. I have a vivid memory of my father in October stuffing toilet paper in the cracks around the windows to try to save fuel. His salary when I was a little boy was three thousand dollars a year. On that he kept a carriage horse, and we lived in this extremely comfortable house, in a comfortable way. He put half of it away and bought a farm with it. I don't know how this was done. My mother must have been cooperative, though. She was not frugal like his family, but she was careful.

My brother lost his leg when he was five years old, when I was only a baby. My mother's sister came by the house one day in a horse and carriage and stopped in front on her way to do an errand of some kind and my mother came out to talk to her. My older brother asked my aunt if he could go with her, and she said no, but he began to climb up the wheel to get in with her anyway and she didn't see it. When she finished the conversation and flicked the whip, his leg slipped down into the wheel and was broken. What happened is that the family doctor was a drug addict. In those days they dispensed their own drugs, so he had access to morphine or whatever. It was a simple fracture that anybody could have set and that would have been the end of it. But he didn't set the leg at all and gangrene set in and they had to cut it off.

Interviewer: This is a secret that you were asked to keep from your brother, according to one thing you have written. Is that fact or fiction?

Maxwell: It's true. I assume he never found out. It wasn't a subject I ever discussed with him because he couldn't bear for anybody to pity him. And people didn't because he was so accomplished physically. He could do wonderful things. He won the tennis championship, the singles, when he was in Scout camp, with his wooden leg dragging across the court. He played football. I saw him once climb up to the high diving board and jump off. What took more courage than the physical part of it was that in his bathing suit, his poor stump was exposed. He faced up to that, did a nice dive and that was that. He was a very brave and remarkable boy.

Interviewer: What about your other brother? Your mother, as is well known because of your work, died of the Spanish flu in the big epidemic in 1918 when you were ten, two days after giving birth to your younger brother. From what I can discern, you use your older brother time and again in your work, but you don't seem to write much about the younger brother.

Maxwell: We weren't with each other very much. My mother's sister said that my mother's dying words were, "I don't want the Maxwells to have my baby." My mother's other sister wanted to adopt him, but my father wanted to bring up his own children. He did his very best. He had a series of housekeepers, which was very hard. His life after my mother died hardly bears thinking about, it was so sad. After two and a half or three years he remarried and his second marriage was, I think, as happy as his first. But in the meantime, while my little brother was small, he

"I wanted a Ph.D. from Harvard because I liked the fact that their robes were lined with scarlet."

spent a good deal of time with my grandmother, my father's mother. She became so attached to him that through one thing or another he spent several days a week with her. Then when he was about three, my father got a promotion and was moved to the Chicago office, which meant we had to leave Lincoln. My grandmother threw herself on her knees and said, "Will, it will kill me if you take this child away from me." He didn't have the heart to do it. So, my brother grew up in a different household and I don't have the daily memories that I have of living with my older brother who shared the same room with me while we were growing up.

Interviewer: You first went to college at the University of Illinois, and then you thought that you wanted to be a professor, so you went on to graduate school. Is that right?

Maxwell: It wasn't quite that simple. I really, from childhood, meant to be an artist. In high school I took art classes, and I was enrolled in the Art Institute in Chicago when I finished high school. But my best friend in school had been a lifeguard during the summer, and he caught pleurisy. His father and mother were afraid to let him go off to school—he was enrolled in Urbana, at the University of Illinois—because they didn't think he was well enough. I said "I'll go down with him, and we can stay in my older brother's fraternity house." Which we did. In the end I didn't want to leave my friend, and I thought the campus looked so exciting. I stayed that freshman year, and in the course of the year I met a very persuasive English teacher, who said, "An artist's life is very uncertain, and a professor's life is pleasant and guaranteed. Why don't you do that?" In the end I decided to be an English professor.

"I was given a room in what had once been a water tower."

Interviewer: Then what did you do?

Maxwell: I graduated from the University of Illinois and went to Harvard for a year. I wanted a Ph.D. from Harvard because I liked the fact that their robes were lined with scarlet. But I had a block on the German language. I think it was because when I was a little boy the papers were full of cartoons of Belgian women with their hands cut off and children on bayonets. I had no trouble learning French or Greek or Italian, not too much trouble with Latin, but with German a total inability to memorize the vocabulary. I plugged along, taking things I liked and could manage, like Medieval French literature, and then began to teach freshmen by way of earning a living. After about two years I read a very lightweight novel called *One More Spring*. It was about some people during the Depression who decided money was not what they wanted and lived happily in a toolhouse in Central Park. For one reason or another it gave me the impetus to throw off the traces, and I resigned my teaching job at Urbana in 1933 or 1934, at a time when there were no jobs anywhere, in the whole United States. And I began to write.

Interviewer: Why? What happened?

Maxwell: Nothing is ever simple, of course. As a graduate student I lived in the house of a woman who was on the English faculty. She had lived in New York and been on the staff of the *Herald Tribune* book section under Stuart Sherman. She belonged to the outside world, really, not academic life. She had a friend who was a History professor at Yale. And he sent her—it seems very odd—he wanted a forty-page condensation of a two-volume life of Thomas Coke of Holcomb, who was a great agriculturist and also

---

William Maxwell

a member of Parliament who introduced the bill to recognize the American colonies. These books arrived, and my friend asked me to take on the job with her. She was interested in the agricultural parts and I was not. So I got to do the rest about social life in the eighteenth century. Coke had an aunt named Lady Mary Coke, who was an object of scandal. Her husband was a boor, and instead of putting up with it, she divorced him. She must have had money, because she continued to live in style. She corresponded with Horace Walpole and dressed her servants in pea-green and silver, and when she was melancholy she used to fish for goldfish in the ornamental pond. She suffered from the delusion that the Empress Maria Theresa was trying to take her servants away from her. In her old age she slept in a dresser drawer. I found all this irresistible. When that job was done I sat down to write a novel.

Interviewer: Where did you go?

Maxwell: I had worked as a boy at a farm in Wisconsin that was not an ordinary farm, but more like the farm in *The Cherry Orchard*, and I began to write the novel while I was actually staying there. I was given a room in what had once been a water tower, but was remodeled. On the first floor there was a room with a piano, for Josef Lhevinne, the great Russian pianist, who used to come there. On the second floor was his bedroom, and on the third floor was a little study with a fireplace, and a chaise lounge and chintz curtains, a very pleasant place among the treetops, and I would sit there writing this book. Several of the characters were just various aspects of me. It was the story of a black man coming to spend a weekend among white people. It was meant to be a comic novel, and it is funny, I guess, in places, but the trouble is, the black man is no good. I finished the novel that summer, and one of my professors at Illinois had a sister who had worked in publishing. She sent it to Harpers, and they took it. That was the beginning.

Interviewer: *Bright Center of Heaven.*

Maxwell: Yes.

Interviewer: In an essay you wrote about E.B. White, you said that when he went West as a young man, he was approaching his destiny by going as far as he could in the opposite direction. You eventually went to New York, and it seems to me that in going East you were approaching your destiny by going as far as you could in the opposite direction as well. Your heart's material is home, the Middle West.

Maxwell: That's perfectly true. In those days the literary world was so strongly centered in New York. When I was at Harvard I'd seen New York and liked it very much. The first time I tried to get a job there I failed because there were no jobs, and my letters of introduction usually ended in the person I had a letter to crying on my shoulder. The second time I got a job with Paramount Pictures, reading novels and writing a summary that would indicate whether they were good material for the movies. Meanwhile I'd had interviews. I'd gone to the *New Republic* where I had an introduction. They soon found out that I didn't know anything about politics. Then I had an introduction to *The New Yorker*, which had published one of my stories. It just happened that Wolcott Gibbs was tired of seeing artists and wanted to extricate himself from the job. I came at a fortunate time, job-hunting.

Interviewer: Your job was to judge the art coming in?

Maxwell: No. Just to deal with the artists. They brought their work in on Tuesday. There was an art meeting later that day. The decorative "spots" were looked at on Wednesday and the artists came back on Thursday and you told them what was bought and what wasn't bought.

Interviewer: By artists you mean....

Maxwell: Cartoonists. And the cover artists, the spot artists. The cartoonists were always respected as very good artists.

Interviewer: So that was your first job at *The New Yorker*.

Maxwell: Yes. I had an interview with Mrs. E.B. White who was the fiction editor and art editor. In the course of the interview she asked me how much money I would want. I had been told that if I didn't ask for thirty-five dollars a week they wouldn't respect me. I took a deep breath and said, "Thirty-five dollars a week." She smiled and said, "I expect you could live on less." And I could have lived on ten quite easily.

"I had been told that if I didn't ask for thirty-five dollars a week they wouldn't respect me."

Interviewer: What year was this?

Maxwell: Nineteen-thirty-six. That night I had dinner in a Chinese restaurant and they wouldn't let me have a table to myself. I was feeling low. Summarizing trashy novels (twenty-five pages minimum, five carbons, payment five bucks) didn't seem a life worth living. I thought, "There's no place in the world for me. Absolutely no place." I went home to the rooming house and under the door was a telegram that said *Come to work on Monday at the salary agreed upon.* I think if you absolutely hit bottom there's nowhere to go but up.

Interviewer: What was the salary agreed upon?

Maxwell: Thirty-five dollars a week. I paid thirty-five dollars a month for a one-bedroom apartment. And you could get a very decent meal at the Automat with lamb chops and baked potatoes and salad and dessert for a dollar.

Interviewer: I take it that at this point you needed to have a day job to support your writing.

Maxwell: I'm pretty sure I could never have supported myself by writing because I was too slow and too much of a perfectionist. The first novel had been published with pleasant reviews. They published a thousand copies and it went into a second edition, printed but only sold a hundred of that second thousand. The rest were all remaindered. I sat down and began a second novel, which was *They Came Like Swallows.* It isn't a very long novel. I did the first section seven times, most of it at that farm in Wisconsin. The eighth time I was at the McDowell colony, and that time it stuck.

"Ross had a map of what was possible to publish in The New Yorker—*wherever, presumably our readers went was what the fiction had to be about."*

It was in the hands of the publisher when I went to *The New Yorker*. It was a Book-of-the-Month-Club choice, to my profound astonishment. The first payment was eight-thousand dollars, which was so much money that I went into Wolcott Gibbs' office to tell him and could hardly walk, stunned by the overwhelming sum.

Interviewer: That was a lot of money at the time.

Maxwell: It was a lot of money. All the time that I was working as an editor I was writing, and the stories were published as a rule in *The New Yorker*, except that people kept resigning ahead of me, so that I kept getting promoted, and doing more and more demanding work, so that I wrote less and less.

Interviewer: At the beginning of *All the Days and Nights*, you tell a story about yourself at the age of twenty-five, which must have been that first time that you went to New York, trying to get on board a ship to be a sailor because you had read that that's really what you ought to do, to go out and get some experience. If you wanted to be a writer, you went to sea first.

Maxwell: Preferably on a four-masted schooner.

Interviewer: Right. To learn to write. You said that at that time, "Three-fourths of the material I would need for the rest of my writing life was already at my disposal." I would like to know, when did you discover that?

Maxwell: I don't remember whether I had written *They Came Like Swallows*, which was of course that material, or was about to. For a long while I was writing stories for *The New Yorker* that were sometimes about New York, sometimes about France. I couldn't write about the Middle West really because Ross had a map of what was possible to publish in *The New Yorker* in fiction. The stories could be about Florida, they could be about Hollywood, they could be about the East Coast—wherever, presumably, *New Yorker* readers went was what the fiction had to be about. Which rather tied my hands, and was a good thing. Because when I was free to write about the Middle West—eventually, after he was gone, they did accept stories about the Middle West—I was old enough to deal with the material. It was as if that was really my imagination's home.

Interviewer: You have been quoted as rejecting the idea of there being a *New Yorker* style or school of writing. And yet, what little I've managed to read about the kinds of restrictions, and the things you've just mentioned, would tend to belie that denial on your part.

Maxwell: Not seriously. I think if there is something characteristic of *New Yorker* fiction, it's that tendency to eliminate the dead spots. Also, for the story to proceed sentence by sentence, and not paragraph by paragraph. You can write fiction just as well in which you make your point in the course of a paragraph. In *New Yorker* writing you make it every sentence, and before you go on to the next one you've made the point in that one. It's very economical.

Interviewer: And yet John Cheever and John O'Hara—two writers closely associated with *New Yorker* fiction—both insisted that the stories they would write they would write for *The New Yorker*, and if you wouldn't take the bloody things they couldn't get anybody else to take them. I think they were saying that they wrote them with *The New Yorker* in mind, and if *The New Yorker* wouldn't take them, there was nobody else publishing that type of fiction. Was it the length? That *The New Yorker* was always publishing longer stories, perhaps?

Maxwell: They slowly got longer. When I first went to work there twelve pages was considered a very long story. Eventually it got up to fifty pages, or even a whole novella. It took a long while.

Interviewer: In talking about the three-quarters of all the material you needed for the rest of your writing life, was the other fourth a matter of learning the trade, the craft, and learning to recognize the right material?

Maxwell: Yes. It takes a while before you know how to deal with your material. I remember once having a conversation with Irwin Shaw over the fact that I was taking such a long time over a novel. He said he always made an outline for his novels and then just did it. I would begin with a metaphor, really. The metaphor for *They Came Like Swallows* was a stone thrown into a pond making a circle, and then you throw a second stone and it makes a circle inside the first circle, as it's getting bigger, and then you throw another stone inside those other two. I made the novel on that structure. In *The Folded Leaf* I saw myself walking across flat territory, such as you'd find in eastern Colorado, toward the mountains. I knew that when I got to the suicide attempt I would have the novel. That's where the heart of the novel was. So I just kept kept getting closer to the mountains by creating scenes. I never wrote an outline for any novel. Sometimes I would run into serious trouble. In *Time Will Darken It* I couldn't decide whether the hero went to bed with the young woman from Mississippi or not, so I wrote it both ways, and continued to write it both ways, chapter after chapter after chapter. It was like a fork in the road. I finally faced the issue and decided that in the year 1912, he wouldn't have. So I threw away all the rest of it. It was a wasteful way of going about it, but I had to discover the form from the material. I didn't have a clear idea, usually, of what I was up to.

Interviewer: When you speak of yourself as a child there are always these wonderful scenes where people are driving in a carriage out in the country. And you've said that as a boy you always loved houses. Do you have any thoughts about the mix of the town and the country as an important element in your writing life?

Maxwell: I've always lived in New York City a very circumscribed life and tried to lead the life I would have if I'd lived in Lincoln. This was not particularly a conscious determination, it's just that I grew up in a small town and it marked me for life. The love of home is I suppose partly because I had it taken away from me. But I loved it before it was taken away from me just as much. We've lived for more than fifty years now in a place in the country—I've lived partly in New York City and partly in northern Westchester—and the place in the country was not built by us. It

"I think what my father gave me was a trust in life."

---

was one of the very early prefabricated houses. After I married my wife began to do something about its box-like nature. Every time we had a child we remodeled the house to make room for the child. Little by little it came to fit our family life, as it was at that time. I know that it isn't practical for either of my children to live there, and it wouldn't be for my wife after I died. Somebody else is going to live in that house. But it's painful. I don't mind dying. I just don't want to leave the house ever. I'm so deeply attached to home.

Interviewer: How did you meet your wife?

Maxwell: She came to *The New Yorker* office looking for work. She wanted to be a poetry editor. She loved poetry. There was no poetry editor as it turned out. She was lovely to look at, but I was in analysis, and at sort of that standstill state that you get in therapy. I did take her telephone number—I guess I just automatically took it. A year later I sat up in the middle of the night and looked her name up in the phone book and it wasn't there. Then I went to the files in the office and it was there. I trumped up some excuse to see her, because I had never forgotten her. She was indeed very beautiful.

Interviewer: You were already living in the country as a bachelor before you married.

Maxwell: Yes. I moved to the country so I could garden and rented a house in Yorktown Heights. I remember sitting and being conscious of the darkness outside the windows. I'd lived in the country before but always with other people, and it was very black outside the window. Then I moved from one rented house to another until the present one.

"If anybody loves you a lot, there's a small piece of ground to stand on."

Interviewer: All in the same area?

Maxwell: All in the same road, within half a mile.

Interviewer: You've spoken of the "sublime confidence" that you must have in order to write a novel. I wonder too if that couldn't be courage. The picture you've painted of yourself is of the over-sensitive kid, the second son, the one who wasn't his father's son; you were the mother's child. Yet what you've done with the material of your life—the kind of exposure that you've subjected yourself to—seems astonishing to me, the courage that it must take to use this kind of material in your fiction.

Maxwell: I've never seen it like that, but I have learned that I am my father's child as much as I am my mother's. When I was six years old we went to Bloomington, which was thirty miles away, where my mother's sister lived. There was a park, and in the park was a lake. You could rent bathing suits and swim. My father, in his bathing suit and I in mine went into the water, and he taught me to swim by putting me on his hand, my face down in the water. I had absolute trust in him, so far as anything of that kind was concerned. I knew that if he said something he would do it. He wouldn't play tricks on me. He told me how to move my arms and legs, what to do. I did what he told me to and suddenly had a moment of doubt. I looked back and he was standing thirty feet away from me in the water, smiling. I think what my father gave me was a trust in life. I don't think it's courage, so much as just trust in life. The only danger is not to do what you want to do. Courage—I certainly don't have much physical courage.

William Maxwell

Interviewer: But your material, the work, is the inner life laid bare—your grief as a child.

Maxwell: I think this is the motivation behind a great deal of fiction—I didn't want the things that I loved, and remembered, to go down to oblivion. The only way to avoid that is to write about them.

Interviewer: There's a piece of yours that was reprinted in *All the Days and Nights*—"The Front and the Back of the House," I think it's called. The story is that you approached an African-American woman who had worked for your parents when you were a little kid, and you hugged her and she rejected you. This hurt and haunted you, and you couldn't figure out what was going on.

Maxwell: It wasn't so much that she rejected me as that she didn't move. It was like hugging a fencepost—the total absence of any response was distressing.

Interviewer: But the point seems to be that in this piece you confront, for the first time, the fact that you've made a fictional world out of your childhood and your life, and that you had no intention at all, in *Time Will Darken It*, of drawing the housekeeper, Rachel, from this woman. And yet, she had read the book and thought you had, and she was very offended by the material in the novel, that wasn't at all her—this rotten husband who was abusive, and in fact trying to abuse her daughter so that she had to go away.

Maxwell: When I look at it now, to save my life I can't always decide which is real and which is imaginary. As I got older I came to have such a respect for life and to believe that the way things actually happened really couldn't be improved on. Even the names of people can't be improved on. So I began to change less and less, and this involved writing more and more about real people, but of course by that time they were mostly dead. I tried to protect them if there was anything that I thought would be painful to them. Sometimes I suffered the torments of the damned about describing real people—where I was sure that I was perhaps causing pain. But in this struggle, the artist won out. There was a point at which I would not give up something which I knew was right aesthetically.

Interviewer: In that particular piece it's as though it had never dawned on you that anybody back home read your books.

Maxwell: I was under the impression that they didn't. They do read them more now, but in those days they didn't very much. A few friends of the family put their name on the list at the public library; but I think in general they didn't read books, so why should they read mine?

Interviewer: A lot of writers say that when you do draw characters from real life, they never recognize themselves. In the case of this woman, who in real life was Hattie, it hadn't been her and yet she thought it was. Has this often proved the case with you?

Maxwell: Sometimes. In *The Folded Leaf* I first described Lymie Peters as having a father and a stepmother. I used my father and stepmother and their social life as a background because it was so incongruous with him, temperamentally. And then I thought, this really isn't fair, my father isn't a literary man and he really won't like being in a book. So I made him a sporting character instead, which my father was definitely not. When I went home, a friend of the family said, "Why did you make your father like that?" People want to identify characters with actual people.

Interviewer: To refer again to your statement that a novel requires "sublime confidence," where did William Maxwell get that confidence?

Maxwell: Long after my mother was dead I took my wife home for a visit and we went to see one of my mother's friends, who was ill. She'd known me ever since I was a small child, and she said, "Your mother told me one day, 'I have such confidence in Billy.'" I was so startled, because I was a very small child, frail and given to tears. Where was this confidence? What was the basis for her having confidence in me? I have no idea. In general, I think confidence has to have come from being loved. She kept me alive by loving me so much. If anybody loves you a lot, there's a small piece of ground to stand on. So maybe that's it.

Interviewer: It wasn't a matter, then, of learning your craft as time went on? Were you more confident with each novel that you wrote?

"The more unconventional it seemed to have to be, the more pleased I was with how things were going."

Maxwell: No. I've never known what I was doing. Only the feeling that the material is in the end your friend, if you give yourself up to it entirely. For example, when I had the idea for *So Long, See You Tomorrow*, what floored me immediately was the fact that I had never lived on a farm. My father had a farm and we went to it occasionally when I was a little boy, but the farmer's children stood off to one side and I was shy and they were shy. I never played with them. I don't think I ever even went inside the house. I saw farmers, but I never lived on a farm. It bothered me so much that I spent a whole year looking at photographs, reading books about farmers' lives, to get inside this closed place. Then one day I thought, "Oh, well. I can trust my imagination, I can go ahead. I know enough." And I did, to my surprise.

Interviewer: In *So Long, See You Tomorrow*, you've plowed into a narrative method that flies in the face of all the conventions in literature that at least your generation believed in.

Maxwell: I had to follow the material. As you get older you take more chances, of course. The more unconventional it seemed to have to be, the more pleased I was with how things were going. It was a hard novel to write. I used to find that sometimes in a paragraph there would be one good sentence and the rest was worthless. So I would cut out the good sentence and put it in a folder. I would say that in a large part of that novel every sentence had been ten other places before it settled down and locked into place. It was much, much, much worked over.

Interviewer: By this time, when you were writing *So Long, See You Tomorrow*, we had seen the surge in what was called parajournalism, with Truman Capote's *In Cold Blood*, and all the work Norman

"The novelist has a moral obligation not to leave the reader with unanswered questions."

Mailer did in that form. Now it's like time has come round to meet you at last. We just call it fine prose, and people teach classes in "creative non-fiction." Were you ever affected by these kinds of things with respect to your choice of form?

Maxwell: Did I worry? Oh, sure. I've worried many many times over novels. I worried most over *The Chateau*, I think, because I was afraid it wasn't a novel at all. I did worry about the structure, and think, "What you're doing you really can't do." Nevertheless I went on and found a way to do it.

Interviewer: We haven't talked about *The Chateau*. You say that you weren't even sure that it was a novel?

Maxwell: Yes. I was afraid it was a travel diary because it followed so closely the experiences of my wife and me during a four-month period in France in 1948. It was a novel in which nothing more profound happened than hurt feelings. I put all the ideas I had for this book on a sheet of paper and tacked it on the bookcase behind me, and never looked at it during the ten years that I was working on the novel. After I'd been working maybe nine years, the Irish short story writer, Frank O'Connor, who wrote for *The New Yorker* and who had become a dear friend, came to the country with his wife and asked how I was getting on with the book. I said, "I'm not getting anywhere. I have a grocery carton full of various versions." He said, "I'd like to read it." I was horrified. I wasn't in the habit of showing my raw material to anybody. On the other hand, as his editor I had seen his rough drafts for what I think is a masterpiece, *An Only Child*. I couldn't very well say, "It's all right for me to see your rough drafts but you can't see mine." So he drove off with the grocery carton, and he and his wife read through all the versions. Then he wrote a perfectly wonderful letter in which he said he didn't understand what I was up to. But in the course of the letter he assumed that it was a novel; he didn't assume that it was a travel diary at all. What he said was, it was really two novels. A great weight fell off my shoulders. I thought, "If it's two novels, anybody can make them into one." So I did.

Interviewer: That book has been compared, I think terribly superficially, to Henry James: the American innocents meeting the deep, dark European decadence. One of the ways that comparison is really not so remote is the fact that you are willing to fly in the face of what was the current convention about narrative method. What I find so remarkable about your work is the confidence with which you just dispense with those kinds of expectations. At the very end, in the epilogue, you just flat out address the reader directly about what was really going on here. You set up a dialogue between the persona and the reader at the end.

Maxwell: What happened was that I reached the end of the narrative, but there were a lot of questions that weren't answered. I felt that the novelist has a moral obligation not to leave the reader with unanswered questions. The problem is then how to answer the questions if the novel is already over. I had a dear friend who read the manuscript through the first part because I needed somebody to tell me when the French people were speaking as French people would. I knew how to have the characters speak bad French, but I wanted to be sure about the good French. He read the novel and had some objections to it. He didn't like the Americans very much and thought they were kind of silly. So he gave me an imaginary person to talk to; I answered some of his objections in this thing, but it also set up the idea of a dialogue.

I loved doing the epilogue. But when it got to the publisher, a man named Harold Strauss, who was then an editor at Knopf, objected to it and wanted to cut it off. I am always so tired when I finish a book that I'm oversusceptible to other people's ideas, and I didn't really know whether it was a good idea or a bad idea. Alfred Knopf was sitting in the room not saying anything, and I turned to him. He said, "Have it the way you want it." So I did. Now, if I were to pick up *The Chateau* and that epilogue wasn't there, I think I would shoot myself.

Interviewer: It is tiresome, isn't it, that every time you have a novel where you have Americans going to Europe and stumbling their way through things and only finding out later what was really going on, inevitably people compare it to Henry James.

Maxwell: With James of course they were high moral dilemmas, and in my case they were social dilemmas, really. Many years later we went to have dinner with the French family, and the deaf woman, who was by then in her nineties and lying on a chaise lounge in a Paris apartment, said sweetly, "You know you were very naughty to write that book. Because you didn't speak French, you didn't understand things." Behind me I heard a whisper from her son-in-law: "He got everything right." It was very gratifying. I suffered the torments of the damned about what it might do to them, since so much of it is taken directly from their lives. I refused to let the book be published, not only in France but in England because I thought English books would get across the channel so easily. I didn't want to hurt them. Eventually they got hold of a copy and read it, and I had a letter from one of them. She said, "It was very naughty of you. Could we please have a copy ourselves?" The last time I saw them, I said, "A long, long time has passed. Is it all right to publish the book in France?" I'd had many offers for it. They said, "We'll read it again." So they read it again and the answer came back, "No, not now. Not ever."

YOU THINK I CARE / *Deborah Way*

ANNIE SEES THE MAN before he sees her.
　　She's on her way to Eric's. A four-point-seven-mile walk. Her mom and dad, as she was leaving, stopped their Saturday-in-November yard work and gave her the ritual I-spy. She had Marlboros in her pocket and a joint snuggled in her sock, but there were leaves to rake and chrysanthemums to pinch, and her mom and dad are never quite so KGB in daylight, and today, especially, you could tell they wanted to trust her—it's the kind of red-cheeked, blue-sky autumn day that makes them want to believe in their daughter's goodness. In the end, they let her go with just a "Be home in time for dinner," and "Be careful on Lawton Pond Road." Annie nodded. Whatever. She's fifteen and in love, and today's the day she and Eric are going to do it.

She'd been planning to ride her bike, but the very last thing her dad said as she was leaving was, "You don't want to ride that bike like that." The shrieking brakes, he meant. "Just wait," he said. "Five minutes. We'll fix it right up." Annie turned around, wheeled the bike into the garage, came back out and said, "I'm walking." She's had enough of those "five minutes" to last a lifetime. Standing there while her dad fixes. He's a banker. He likes to think he's handy.

"Here," he says. "Hold this." "Hand me that wrench." "Learn something new. It's good for you." Annie's learning just fine. She's getting hundreds in Algebra Two and A-pluses in English, and even, in Biology, A's, which could be A-pluses because Eric's been stealing the tests, but why be greedy; why tempt fate?

And then her mom would come around to watch them work on the bike, and pretty soon she'd be giving Annie the eye, shaking her head and saying, "Two closets full of clothes, and you can't find something halfway decent." And her mom would look at her dad, and her dad would say, "She's right. You don't want to go out dressed like that."

"You can't read in that light."

"You don't."

"You can't."

Normally, Annie would say, "Watch me." But today—the idea of riding off on her bike after that—it just seemed like all the way to Eric's she'd be steaming, poisoned, it would maybe bring her bad luck. Today of all days she needs good luck. Eric's parents are in Peru, and they'll have the house to themselves and, please, she's already into her second pack of pills; she's spent how many Friday and Saturday nights naked with Eric in his bed, and she's tried, and he's tried—if she can't do it today, when will she ever?

It's an old road, Lawton Pond Road, narrow and twisting, the kind of road where, if you're Annie's parents, you're tapping the horn every other minute because you can't see around the next curve. The kind of road, too, where, at least in southeastern Pennsylvania, there aren't many houses, because the ones there are, are super-fancy, with property up the butt: manicured grounds that turn to picturesque fields that turn to woods, acres and acres. The kind of houses you're never sure if people really live in because even now, in November, when the trees are half-bare and you *could* see, you never do see anyone around.

The man, when Annie spots him, is doing something to the passenger-side door of a junky old boat-sized American car—both of them, man and car, looking not exactly like what you'd expect in the driveway of what used to be a stone farmhouse but now is some super-rich family's home. It has bushes neatly covered with burlap, all cozy and tucked in for winter. It has a garage, brilliant white, that used to be a barn; one of the double doors is open; there's a green Jaguar inside.

The man is older, in his thirties at least, Annie can tell even from down the road. It's a thickness about him—something set that wouldn't be if he were younger.

Annie's going to have had many lovers by the time she's that old. It's *not* that she wants to stay a virgin; the word itself—she can hardly think it, it gives her such creeps. She hates that whole idea of girls having something to *lose*. And the boys at school who talk like it's theirs to take—yuck, clowns—she's fooled around with them, shivering on the grass in someone's backyard, being poked and rubbed and squeezed until she wants to scream. Sometimes it's rained, and always she's sick about slugs maybe waiting to touch her.

Eric Benson is the one, bringing her inside to his bedroom, a miracle worth the climb onto the roof and in through his window, worth the ride home in a creepy cab. If her parents only knew. They drop her off at his house; they think the Bensons bring her home.

Duh. The Bensons. The Bensons never even know she's there. Eric never locks his bedroom door. He likes to torment Annie. *You forget!* he says. And waves his hand—abracadabra—like it's Eric-magic keeping Mrs. Benson at the piano and Professor Benson in his study, admiring his Pre-Columbian art. They've never even asked Eric what he knows about the ladder propped up against the back of the garage.

Annie doesn't mind the ladder. What she hates is getting from the ladder to the roof, that moment when there's nothing to grab but she clutches anyway, scrabbling at the shingles like some kind of rodent. It's lucky Eric's never there to see, because she doesn't need a mirror to know her fear is u-g-l-y. He'd have to look away.

The man nods when he sees Annie looking.

She turns her head, quickly, and keeps walking, keeping her eyes on the ground until she's past him. For a minute she thought he was going to offer her a ride, and, oh, that makes her heart pound, because she'd have refused, no question. But then he could have followed her, and who'd have stopped him? The trees? It kills her: you look at someone and he acts like that's an invitation. How could anyone think Annie would be dumb enough to say yes? Can't you see in her eyes that she's headed for Harvard? Does she not seem like a person who had parents, and teachers, and Officer Whoever who gave a safety talk at school the year the Flasher was hanging around? Does she not seem like all her life people have been telling her, "Never take rides from strangers?"

She does, of course, take rides from strangers, if you count the cabs she takes home from Eric's. Nothing's stranger than that. It still surprises her, hurts her even, that she should have to pay to ride in dirty, falling-apart cars—which is what the cabs are, just disgusting cars. No light-thing on the roof. No phone number on the side. It's not like TV, not New York. The cabs aren't even yellow. They're just stickiness and lint and vinyl seats with strange eruptions.

They make good stories for Eric, though, and even for Annie there's something great about them, about thinking of herself as so not-squeamish, like what does any of it matter, it's just her body, one machine riding in another. But that feeling always comes later. In the cabs, at night, in the dark, after Eric's, Annie wishes she weren't any part body, she wants to float, touching nothing, no eyes to see the driver with the skinniest neck in the world, no ears to hear the one who grunted all the way home. And the last one, who had his piggish girlfriend with him, practically on his lap. Annie had to make herself breathe.

And then here is the man, right beside her, in the Jaguar, driving walking-speed on the wrong side of the road.

"Need a lift?" he asks.

Without missing a step, Annie looks him in the eye and says, "No, thanks." He has brown hair, cut short, no glasses, no mustache, no scars, at least none she can see.

"You're sure," he says.

Annie doesn't answer. A car is coming the other way. If the man notices, he doesn't care; he stays right next to her, on the left side of the road, and the car has to swerve to miss him. It's two girls, probably not much older than Annie. As they pass, they're yelling: "Suck my ass! Learn to fucking drive!" Annie wants to run after them and say it's not her fault; she's never seen this man before in her life.

From the expression, the non-expression, on his face, you'd think he hadn't heard the girls. He just keeps driving, four miles an hour, hardly taking his eyes off Annie to make sure he's staying on the road.

"You like walking," he says.

"I like walking." Is it her, is it something about her? Is her mother right about the clothes?

"It's okay, you know," the man says. "I live here. I mean, my family does. I'm visiting."

He's smiling, sort of, like You poor funny thing. Annie's ears are burning. Why would he say that, about living here? Truth or dare? It hadn't occurred to her that he honestly might not have belonged back at that house, but now that he brings it up, who knows? He could have stolen the Jaguar. The rusty other car could have been his. Because look at him: he's dressed like an attendant. All that's missing is the embroidered name.

But look at Annie, twenty minutes ago, back in her driveway. You could have said she didn't belong either, with her jeans ripped all the way across her butt and her sweater on backwards because the front has holes and Annie never wears a bra.

And another thing: Annie lies, and Eric steals tests, but she'd never tell a lie that big and he'd never steal a car, especially a Jaguar, in broad daylight with the house right there. Didn't she notice lights on in the hosue, and wasn't smoke coming out the chimney?

She stops walking to light a cigarette, to see if the car will stop, too. It keeps going, still at walking speed. Annie fishes for matches. She should be relieved, and she is. And yet—it's like when you get off a roller-coaster, and the whole time you were on it you thought you'd puke, but when it stops, you think, That's it? She wishes she'd worn sunglasses so she could stare without the man knowing—*if* he's watching her in the rearview mirror, which she'd bet anything he is.

As she's striking the match, the car stops. Thirty, maybe forty feet away. It's like Simon Says. Annie can hardly light the cigarette her hands are shaking so—from fear, yes, but even more from the sudden, amazing understanding that she, Annie, a fifteen-year-old girl, is the one in complete control. Simon Says, "Stop."

Her heart is racing, pounding faster than it does on Eric's roof. It's her choice. She can get in the car. She can see herself there. It could be his car; he could be visiting. It's got Delaware plates: RLR-243.

There was a joke when she was little: Annie's mom said, "Will Delaware her New Jersey?" Annie said, "Idaho, Alaska."

If he wants to be her ride, let him come to her. She has a cigarette; she can burn him; what's the worst he can do? Let him back up and ask her again.

The Jaguar, on the inside, is cleaner, if that's possible, than Annie's dad's Continental. So immaculate, so pristine, that Annie drops her cigarette before getting in.

"Where to?" the man asks.

"End of this road," Annie says, and wishes she didn't sound so breathless, "and then right and then the first left." She waits for a joke about the end of the road, but he doesn't make one, just looks at her—at her hair—which is, she knows, one of her best features. Eric says it tastes like auburn; he likes to have some in his mouth when they kiss.

She looks out the window, letting her eyes blur over the trees, over the giant Tudor house that's the last house. After it, there's nothing, just land—woods and fields—and Lawton Pond and the road.

"What's there?" the man asks.

"Where?"

"Where you're going."

"Friend's house," Annie says, and wonders if he can possibly believe her, or if it's obvious that she's on her way to a boy who'll undress her, who'll do things and watch her and whisper, "Do you like it?" wanting her to like it, and she will.

The man is watching her, she can feel it. She can see herself at the line-up, pointing—"That's him"—and the cops congratulating her for having gotten away, for having poked his eyes out with her fingers, smashed his windpipe with the side of her hand, raked her nails down his face so there'd be skin samples, not to mention scars. Not that she's planning to be a victim—just the opposite. It's like setting your alarm clock and then waking up before it goes off. Picturing how she could defend herself means she'll never have to.

She opens her window. "Mind if I smoke?"

"Go ahead," he says. "I'll take a drag."

No, you won't, Annie thinks. She lights two Marlboros and hands him one. As he takes it he brushes his fingers against hers, though there's no need to, she's barely holding the cigarette. She knows the trick. She's done it herself, before she got together with Eric, when passing a joint was her only chance to touch him.

She loves it that this man is trying so hard to connect, and the whole time, to her, he's just a *ride*. She loves a ride, up in the front seat, smoking, what a day to be in a car—this car—she's embarrassed for her poor self who wanted to walk. She can't wait to be at Eric's. Drinking a beer. Telling her story. Adding danger.

"Hey," the man says. "What do you think, is there someplace I can stop and take a whiz?"

Annie wants to laugh—Excuse me?—that's like Eddie Williams in first grade who used to chase her and pull her hair and call her "doo-doo" because, it turned out, he liked her.

She's about to say "I don't know," when it hits her: a person who truly belonged back at that house wouldn't be asking her where to pee. She looks at him and says, "Your house?"

"Shit," he says.

She can't tell if it's *Shit, okay you caught me* or *Shit, I just left there; I don't want to go back.* They're passing Lawton Pond. Three boys—kids—are standing at the edge of the water. They don't look over, and then the car's going around the bend and Annie can't see them anymore.

"Shit," the man says. "I gotta go." And without warning, or asking—one minute he's driving around a bend past where Annie can see the pond, and the next minute he's stopped on the side of the road. Parked. Engine off. Annie braces herself—for what, she's not sure; it's so daylight; she could scream and those pond-boys would come running—but the man just sits there, forever, it seems, smoking his cigarette like he's got all day.

Eric should be back at the pond, waiting, like the night in August when Annie's mom and dad were at a retirement party for some First Valley Bank vice-president and Annie was free to roam.

"Eric," she said. "Meet me." He rode to her on his bike. "I want to go on the Pill," she said. He said "Okay," and kissed her. Not like Oh, my God—just a normal sexy Eric-kiss, telling her they were together and fine, and she turned him on. "Whatever you want," he said. It seemed that easy.

If he were at the pond now, she could get out of the car and not have to worry that she'd panicked for possibly no reason.

The man is stabbing out his cigarette in the ashtray. "I have this thing," he says.

Annie's staring over the dashboard so she can watch him out of the corner of her eye, and he must sense this half-attention because suddenly his hand is between his legs. "Piss-hard," he says. "You know piss-hard?" He turns to face her, and—she can't help it—she turns to face him. It's his voice: so unexpectedly bright, as if he's just discovered their mutual interest—he might have been saying, "You know Pre-Columbian art?" "You know quadratic equations?" He could, for all she knows, know quadratic equations. His eyes are bright, like there's stuff—busy stuff, maybe even smart stuff—going on behind them.

"You know what to do for it?" he says.

For piss-hard, he means? How would she? What is it? Should she?

"You ever felt it?" he says, and then shakes his head. "Probably not. You don't seem the type."

Annie looks away from him, finally, stares at her lap. What type? She wants to tell him "Fuck off."

"Well," he says, "in case you're curious, it's like a rock."

His hand's not moving. If he means he has a boner, why not say so? Maybe she's not even hearing him right. Piss-hard? Piss-heart? She lights a new cigarette off her old one. Is this where nine out of ten girls would run? Or is it just strange, and if she ran, back to the pond, to those boys, they'd turn out to be somebody's little brothers, and in two days everyone, including the man, would be snickering at Annie the overreacting freak.

He's not hurting her, physically. His hand's not even moving. Whatever he's talking about, maybe if she lets him talk, he'll get it out of his system and they can get back on the road and she can forget anything ever happened.

"You can touch it," he says. He reaches for her left hand, her non-smoking hand—it's just sitting in her lap, practically screaming, "Come and get me"; and now she can't move it—it's too late— he'll know that he's got her.

"No," she says, just as he's about to touch her. He pulls his hand away, but instead of starting the car—what you'd think he'd do; he must be mortified; he's learned his lesson, she hopes— instead of turning the key and starting the car, he opens his door and gets out, walks around the front of the car and paces at the edge of the woods, crunching, crackling through the leaves.

Annie could get out. She could start the car and drive. If she could turn the key; if her hands would stop shaking.

The crunching stops. She hears the zipper unzipped. She's not going to watch him pee. If he *can* pee, which maybe he can't, because she's not hearing anything but a blue jay squawking and the clutch of her own throat as she tries to make smoke rings. She wants to send Eric a signal, so he'll think of her suddenly and not know why, but the rings are puffy and indistinct, gone before they're even out the window.

What Annie sees when she looks out the window is the man, with his back to her, and the man's arm, bent at the elbow and moving. Of course. She should have known.

Maybe she did know. Maybe that's why, though she doesn't watch, she continues to sit there, listening to herself breathe, wondering if his eyes are closed, and what, with them closed, he sees her doing.

She wonders if he'll breathe like a monster. In fourth grade, the year the Flasher was hanging around, she and her friend used to do that for fun: sneak up behind an unsuspecting first- or second-grader and breathe at them like a monster. She never saw the Flasher. No one did, even though at recess she and her friends played at the edge of the playground, by the sidewalk and the quiet street. Every figure in the distance gave Annie goosebumps, but it was never him, never even a man. Once they saw a tall old lady who looked like a man, dressed in too-big clothes and swearing to herself. She headed straight for them, swearing down the sidewalk, and just as she passed and everyone was starting to giggle, she turned and said, "Devils!" Someone screamed, and everyone ran, holding hands for safety.

When he gets back to the car, a pine needle is stuck to his sleeve. It spiraled down from the tallest branch of the tallest tree and landed on his sleeve. Annie sees how it happened because she's not really here. She's taking everything in from a dreamy distance: the trees, the pond, the chill in the air, the smell of the air, like a jar of pennies, the road, and on the road, a shiny green car, and in the car, a girl, and a man.

And then they're driving again, coming up on the stop sign at the end of Lawton Pond Road, half a mile, maybe less, from Eric's. He brakes for the stop sign, so smoothly, so gently, the car might have been filled with eggs and not one of them would have broken. Annie opens her door and gets out. Just like that. So easy it makes her want to cry. She's two steps from the car when he calls her. "Hey," he says.

She turns, patting her pockets, expecting from the tone of his voice that she left something, cigarettes or matches.

He's leaning across the seat. Smiling.

"Guess what?" he says. "You think I care if you walk?"

By the time she gets to Eric's, she's sweating all over—clammy November sweat, trickling down her back, beading up between her breasts. She got there by not thinking, by just moving forward. Pitching forward was how it felt, like each clumsy step was postponing her fall.

As she's ringing the doorbell she sees herself in the window in the door. And then the door opens, and there's Eric, grinning, stepping aside to let her in, expecting her to be delighted. Not asking what took her so long. Not noticing that she's bug-eyed and ugly.

She pushes past him. In the mirror in the hall it's worse than she thought: not only is her face entirely sweat-filmed; it's grayish-white, like the inside of a cut potato that's been sitting out on the counter too long.

She heads for the French doors at the back of the kitchen—past black-and-white photos of Eric, in diapers, toddling around archaeological digs; past two-foot-high stacks of Professor Benson's books and papers; past a half-empty pan of brownies, probably pot brownies, probably Eric's breakfast. He's behind her the whole way; he follows her outside.

"Hey!" He's laughing.

She climbs her ladder and sits on the edge of the roof. All the nights she's been up here, she's never noticed the gutter. It's clogged, inches deep with leaves and twigs and nosies, Pinocchio nosies, the name her dad taught her for the maple-tree things you peel open and stick on your nose. The Bensons call them helicopters. Annie's dad would take one look at this gutter and decide the Bensons were no good.

She lights a cigarette. Eric's goofing, grinning his most charming grin, like it's all a game, like it's Valentine's Day and she's slipped him a candy heart that says *Woo Me*.

"I'm not laughing," she says. He's beautiful, standing in the grass in bare feet and jeans and no shirt, only a towel around his neck. His hair is wet. His hair is the same length as hers, to just above the shoulders. He uses cream rinse. She loves him for that. She doesn't want to be mad at him for having just woken up, for having slept while she was getting jerked around, for not having met her halfway. It's not his fault they could never have any privacy at her house.

"Why am I here?" she says.

"Because you're crazy about me and—"

"I don't think so," she says.

He starts climbing the ladder. She stops him with her foot.

"What?" he says.

What can she say? That she sat in a car feeling like she was five again and scared of the dark and the things maybe hiding—wanting to run, to open her mouth and make some noise, but afraid to give herself away?

They stare at each other. Annie's pulse is thudding in her neck. The ladder rung is digging into the backs of her knees.

Of course, she thinks, of course the man cared. It was just to freak her out that he said he didn't. To try to make her think she wanted him to. He cared. Period.

Eric looks away. And shivers.

Annie blows smoke at his face. "Go back in," she says, "if you're so cold."

He lets the door slam.

She starts to get up, to get down, but her feet have fallen

Deborah Way

asleep—which is lucky, after all, because if she did get down, she'd have no choice but to leave. She will not go crawling after him.

She tosses her cigarette into the grass and watches it go out.

The only thing is: if he cared so much, why'd he get out of the car? And turn his back? Isn't the whole point to be seen? Like the Flasher—isn't the point to be seen?

She could go inside and call a cab. But what if Eric didn't stop her?

He must, the man, be so pleased with himself, driving around, laughing out loud. He'll be bragging to his friends: *She asked for it.*

Did she? Ask for it? The Flasher, okay, she wanted to see him, but it's different when you're a kid. She didn't want this other man after her. What kind of girl would want that?

There's a noise behind her. She turns just in time to miss the bottle of beer rolling by—a peace offering from Eric, who's balanced on the peak of the roof. He winces as the bottle smashes on the brick walkway.

"What was it?" Annie asks.

"Nothing," he says. "Miller. But it was the last one."

Before Annie can say anything, apologize or blame, she's crying, and Eric's behind her, holding her, cheek to cheek, smoothing her hair, saying he was kidding, look, he has another one right here.

She can't tell him that's not it, that's not why she's crying. He'd say, Well, why are you? And she wouldn't know how to explain. It's always been like that. Annie's mom, talking about Annie as a baby, says she was a mystery, that she screamed and screamed and nobody, ever, could figure out what she wanted.

"Eric?"

He nods his head against her cheek.

"Let's do it," she says.

He has to help her up. Her feet are heavy—still asleep—it's hard to know where to put them. At the top of the roof, she makes Eric stop, to stand for a minute and kiss. Always, she has hurried past this point, to be inside, away from spying neighbors, out of danger. Strange now, to be lingering, kissing in midair.

Somewhere there's a car and a man who knows.

Annie takes Eric's beer, tilts her head to drink. The sun is warm on her face. Every other time up here, she's been with the moon. There was a rhyme when she was little: *I see the moon and the moon sees me; God bless the moon, and God bless me.* She's whispered that up here, for luck. She's never noticed before how it's not a rhyme—how it's as if, in all the whole wide world, nothing rhymes with *me.*

Deborah Way is our Editors' Prize winner in fiction. This is her first published story.

"WHAT THE HELL IS AN INSTA-BOOK?"

ALTITUDE / *Kathy Fagan*

When smoke rose from the swung censer
   it rose on a choral breath
It rose slowly and in waves
   like the congregants and rode
From vault to vault the nave's
   ceiling where we believed
It found escape
   We believed in transcendence then
As we believe in movies each Christmas
   and from the very first reel
That even the smallest prayer may pass
   through nebular dust to heaven
Where the ratio of angel to living man
   is one to one
Believed as we believe in dreams
   pinned to spots of light above us
And in actions finding answer
   in an out of reach elsewhere
Believed with the belief that drops the "t"
   from constellation when looking toward
The stars Desire is its own pilot
   at this or any season traversing the city
And clouds lit by the city the illumined
   cloudcover like a landscape
Transposed a language made legible
   on buoyant tongues It is not a trick
Of fuel tailings or engine's din but a visible
   sheen an audible innocence
In which the lights of approach and departure
   seem one And as a season's
Rain ticks at our tablet windows
   a mechanization of gears in the belly
Goes round like applause
   among passengers at touchdown

EASTER SUNDAY / *Kathy Fagan*

Church bells, rain, deer
  pellets in the pine
beds, and lichens ecstatic

  for a northern god. All morning
I have waited for a sign
  greater than these: companion

blood, an animate spirit. The body
  of a nuthatch found on my doorstep only
strengthened that need. How light

  it was! A no-weight in my hand,
as hers had been. Then too
  I waited. Believed I would have

gone where she was going
  for a sign. There are at least two
sides of grief: on one,

  you're watchful; the other makes you
turn away. And maybe we don't
  get to choose. Like at the all-you-can-

eat salad bar, the ones whose mothers didn't,
  my friend said, love
them enough, first plates piled

  too high, I looked everywhere:
shadow at my left shoulder, shadow
  on my right. Then mourning

doves on the car-hood. Enclosed
  parking garage. I convinced myself
with that. But what of?

Winter fog in the valley, summer
fog on its grape; and the lightning of spring lanced
in fall's halved tomato.

I once dreamed a city divided
by water. No bridge, no boat, no way across
that I could find. And the dream-

self asked, How will the children
go to school? And her voice answered, surprising
me, answered, Zero Street,

then said no more. Zero,
as in nothing, as in bottom, as in
no-place-you-know

open   closed   whole   gone.
As in open. As in whole.
Leaves young beeches hold all winter

strike low flames through the woods
like chandeliers lit and waiting
to be raised. It is April,

and snow unthawed in the darker reaches
heaves as though someone breathed
beneath it. Three days ago, sun,

and the tap, tap of creepers
round the base of a pine tree. That morning,
they made all the circles they wanted.

VIGIL / *Kathy Fagan*

He was saying how any note struck on the piano that day
    even in error
was enunciated like a syllable from the perfect throat

how a moth applauds smallest
    it prays otherwise

and the saw-whet calls for who
    knows how many nights before
then feeling no need
    it does not call

    like a wick that waits for its flame to come
        (don't make me lonely)
    like a mirror waiting for its face

But I was silt on the lakebed that night
    and she the boat spun on its surface
and though it was already much too dark
    I'll wait for you here was what she said

Here and elsewhere
Her and not

Like a singular crow
    and the pine limb it sits on
        swaying perhaps

Or perhaps it was a tree entire
    conversed with the wind
        that moved it

And then someone mentioned new theory on purpose
It was the theory of original sin
    and had been
    for some millennia

powerlines down
hoses unmanned
and up from the loam
some runners in red
a runner and red leaves
of what

Currents and currents and leaping
connections
all meaning the same as
(don't make me)
lonesome

As a girl I called the hydrangea
hi danger: powdered old women in fragrant green coats
And grandmother used the words
far head for forehead
And of course there's always
euthanasia

Don't do it my friend said
There's no hope in that

It's not prayer otherwise
neither prayer nor piano

All that can fly you see
strictly forbidden

Also anything that does not
fly

Nothing but empty
vesseling there

And we need someone (my flame, my face)
to take it in (don't make me wait)
to take it up and pour it out (I will for you here)
again and again

an alphabet sung
to the pleasure of the child

for the pleasure of the lesson
and listener

Kathy Fagan is our Editors' Prize winner in poetry. She is a former McAfee Discovery Feature poet whose first book, *The Raft*, was a National Poetry Series selection.

THE ONE STRONG FLOWER I AM
/ Donald Morrill

THEY ARE RUNAWAYS, THROWAWAYS, "problem" teens; culls from meager schools and emissaries from questionable homes; bearers of "emotional disabilities" and lurid autobiographies for which they are medicated elaborately and counseled when possible; products of biology, family, community—of fate, impure and hardly simple.

They have landed here, in the group home school, where Sarah, their instructor, and Bob, her assistant, try to give them enough structure and knowledge to function in the working world beyond graduation. In the middle of this task, for two hours each week, I am to teach them to write poetry.

Poetry: a marginalized art form for marginalized people, I think, as I pull into the school parking lot on the day of our first session. I've taken this assignment because I am a poet and have lived into middle age believing the golden assertions of poetry's proponents: that poetry matters because it somehow enlarges the individual imagination, it articulates the life of the soul, it makes the world cohere. I have believed this because I love poetry, but now I suspect my love is rather effete. What place does poetry really claim in this culture, when advertising is the current school of eloquence, and the metaphor of the marketplace devours all other figures of thought? If poetic art is supposed to be so fine for the soul, I wonder, why don't more people care about it, and practice it? Only the fierce grandchildren of the Beats, who dominate poetry slams and spoken-word performances, and coteries of university professors seem interested in it. What would a group of hardening and hurt kids think of a poem? The implication in hiring someone like me is that poetry is only self-expression, and self-expression is therapy—something the suffering and disenfranchised need.

I enter the front door of the school—a seedy starter house from the 1940s in a scruffy working-class neighborhood. The organization that operates the school and several runaway shelters in the area subsists on government grant money; thus, the facilities are humble and the salaries slight enough to attract only the professionally transient or morally committed. Once inside, I see that many of the inner walls have been removed, and all those remaining have been painted a calming pale mauve. I'm introduced to a dozen or so students spread strategically across desks and tables, a map of emotional nation-states, I will learn later, alliances and betrayals.

Frankly, I'm scared, accustomed to the hierarchy of the college classroom where no matter how antagonistic or aliterate the students are, the professor is still endowed with enough symbolic power to make them comply with the day's agenda. But what do I do here if these kids merely sit before me, a Mount Rushmore of indifference?

I keep the formalities short, and the explanations. This is no land for lecturers. Activity—the pen chasing the completion of the assignment across a page—is my hopeful lubricant. I have assignments—exercises gleaned from the cottage industry of textbooks on teaching children to write poetry, from my colleagues and friends who have taught for years in the Poets in the Schools Program. All assure me that these teens will want to write about themselves, so we begin with a poem by Donald Hall, "Self-Portrait, as a Bear." Though two of the students, boys, refuse to write, they do so out of a sedate shyness, preferring to sit quietly while the others work. In minutes, the rest of the class produces self-portraits as manatees, junkyards, great white hummingbirds. It seems simple, natural. Each wants to read his or her poem, and it thereafter becomes our custom to "read around" the room after each writing session. Often arguments and fights erupt over who will read next, though some of the students struggle to articulate their words when their turn arrives. One of them, Becky, becomes so overwrought by the wall between her ability to write words and read them that she throws herself down in her chair and shrieks. Seemingly oblivious to her torment, the class explodes into a flurry of waving hands.

After a while the group senses it is break time, and they scatter into the backyard to shoot baskets while Bob monitors them. Hoping to gauge how I'm doing, I remark to Sarah that the kids seem talented and excited. She is a matter-of-fact woman in her fifties, who will prove wonderfully enthusiastic, but today she is tired. "These kids are worse off now," she says, "than a couple of decades ago. They've got dysfunctional *extended* families. And it's difficult for us to deal with such a mixed bag of students. Some of them are brilliant but emotionally troubled, some are just dull. Others are needing a lot of repair. Some are, I'm afraid, certifiably loony."

The students return, careening and sweating from the court, and it takes a few minutes to settle them. Lee Ann, a glib powerhouse of sixteen, is "cracking" on Jed, a short, doughy boy who is clearly an outcast of the group. All the ridicule is sexual, and Bob tells me later that my sway as the stranger in town helps him cut off the teasing sooner than usual. I then continue with another exercise, using Larry Woiwode's poem, "A Deserted Barn," which begins "I am a deserted barn." They are to replace the barn with their own metaphor.

They write and then read—"I am a VW van," "I am a brain in a jar"—and when it is time for me to go, I'm elated. Though two boys have shied from writing, the rest of us have begun successfully. The group wasn't so threatening, I tell myself. I want to thank them, but a number of the kids have already preoccupied themselves with other activities, peering into a workbook or a computer game. There is no ceremony of parting, as I'd like. I want copies of their poems but I'm unsure about how to ask for them. I'm afraid of these kids, still, afraid to pry and uncertain how much intimacy is allowable. I depart feeling as though I've given of myself honestly, yet I peer back at myself with some unease from the rearview mirror.

The following week I arrive with poems by William Blake for Sid, whose writing from the previous session sounded a little like some of the *Songs of Innocence and Experience*, but Sid has been removed from the program, no explanation given. In his place I find Charles, who has a history of glue-sniffing and marijuana use. He's re-entered the program, arriving from his family home infested with so many lice that his head has been shaved. He looks a little like a detention camp internee, but wears huge, cascading shirts and vast shorts the crotch of which arches just above his knees—a surrounding intentionally too large, I imagine, so he can never grow into it. Over the coming months, he maintains a stupefied gentility, and though I ask him frequently to participate, he declines. Closer to graduation than the other students, he sometimes leans over workbooks he must complete to gain his high school equivalency certificate. Often, he stares absently into space. Sarah tells me that Charles "has come a long way" from being the feral thug who ranted and slugged any face he didn't like. I wonder what he will do after graduation, what kind of clothes he will be able to wear in the world. There is hope, Sarah says, to get him into a trade right away. In the meantime, he becomes a spirit of absence that hovers over the room, the available non-contact.

On this day the talk turns to issues of racism. I've learned already that I must be willing to forgo any lesson plans and adopt some scheme that co-opts the mood of the room, so I decide that we shall read poems by Langston Hughes and Lucille Clifton—which receive only mild interest. All present declare discrimination criminal. They know about being outcasts. And though everyone in this class is white, they know something about people of color since the group homes in which they live are run by two black couples with a loose religious affiliation. Still, the kids line up against each other on the slightest pretext—often based on adolescent sexual cliquism—and they think nothing of verbally stoning one of the group. Of the greater world of issues and movements, of ideas and possibilities and socially-approved ambitions, they are mostly ignorant, corralled by their age and circumstances into a self-involvement at once crucial and, it seems, stunting.

To shift the tone of the session I have them write their version of Wallace Stevens' "Thirteen Ways of Looking at a Blackbird." Sybil, the fifteen-year-old daughter of recovering heroin addicts, drives into the page as she writes. Bob tells me that she has composed many poems on her own. She struggles with her studies and her moods, damaged by her parents' self-abuse. She bragged one day when members of the class boasted about how young they were when they first smoked crack or dropped acid, "Hey, I was born an addict." Still, unlike Charles, she generally exhibits a sturdy work ethic, probably because her father has been pushing her in that direction. He counsels recovering addicts and knows the value of discipline. So, today, Sybil is eager to achieve and move on, diligent no matter how wavering her course. She writes:

Five Ways of Looking at the Left Hand

　　　1.
Plump, the shortest of your kind.

　　　2.
Who are you? Why do you point
so rudely?

　　　3.
Bad, Bad, Bad!
Keep yourself down
you are not wanted!
Don't express yourself.

　　　4.
To be or not to be,

Will you or will you not,
that is the question.

5.

Baby! Baby!
So you are the baby.
Oh, how you depend on your family,
the four of us!

During the read-around, the group begins to unravel. Sarah sees it long before I do, and as soon as possible, she intervenes. She directs the class to a video on the life and poetry of William Carlos Williams. On the stand below the television, titles of cassettes outline the agenda of warning and reform—AIDS, Understanding Your Anger, STDs, Contraception, Gangs.... Sarah says she needs the television to draw the group together. The light of the screen, the action, focuses their attention as no other force can. "It tames them," she says. Though its effect is temporary, they behave better under its watchful eye than under the policing gaze of the institutional point system, an economic paradigm in which instead of money one earns points, and, thus, privileges, for good behavior. As the video concludes, with long passages from Williams' later work—quite beautiful but complex and abstract—I assume we will hear the kinds of remarks sometimes uttered by certain students at my university: "boring," "kinda long." But there is an amazed silence, some of it emanating from visual sedation but some from another source. "That was gorgeous," says Jed, the group pariah, almost sighing. "Really, awesome."

As the weeks unfold and spring bursts forth with the purple blossoms of the jacarandas near the school, the sessions assume their individual shapes yet evolve into a single drama of manifold relations. Each time I approach the house, I look toward the front window to gauge the conditions inside, hoping for a wave or smile. I am met at the door with poems—assigned and written privately— by Jed, Sybil, Tommy and others, and I begin collecting them, though I'm hardly up to the students' enthusiasm, the neediness that is flooding my way. Jed, for instance, begins each session with the question, "What shall I write?" and he lavishes whole hours by himself, working on the first subject I suggest. Bob says that Jed's family scattered and his grandmother cares for him on the weekends, which amounts to her locking him in his room because she fears his rages. Jed tells me that he writes because he plays guitar and wants to start a band. On the computer's auto design game, he fashions a racer for me. It brakes well but is endowed with so much speed, he can't control it. He takes me aside to say he remembers a movie about Walt Whitman, *Beautiful Dreamer*, starring Rip Torn.

Clearly, he craves any kind of male attention, and I try to balance his attachment against the demands of the group and my own desire for emotional elbow room. One day, he notices the fountain pen in my pocket and asks if he can examine it. The pen was moderately expensive, a gift from my wife. I had been advised at my orientation to the program not to bring valuables into the school because they could be stolen easily. "These kids are survivors," the case worker said, "they can be savvy about getting what they want." This is the first day I have forgotten to leave the pen in my car. I hand it to Jed, and he uncaps it with his thick hand, touching the nib to the tip of his index finger. I cringe inwardly, fearing that he will somehow damage it, ashamed that I'm seeing him as some kind of ape holding a glass egg. But he writes his name slowly, delicately. "Boy, I'd sure like to have a pen like that," he says, passing it back to me. He generates poem after poem, probing himself, and I encourage him, undeservedly proud, wondering where his words will lead him, and us.

> When I take off,
> I have a secret place to stay,
> I have a big bush that totally surrounds me,
> I made a bed out of straws,
> I never was seen by anyone,
> I always saw them,
> I sometimes spent all day there,
> It got lonely and sad,
> I had no one to talk to,
> Just like everyday of my life,
> I can smell the leaves and straw,
> I can feel myself get pricked by the straws,
> I get bitten by spiders and ants,
> This is how I feel everyday of my life,
> When I wake up the next
> Morning I feel in pain and sad;
> I feel dirty as a bum,
> Everytime I see a cop car,
> I dive in the bushes,
> I hate that feeling
> of not being liked everyday of my life.

More and more, I try to avoid gestures that mark me "the

teacher." As often as the group can sustain it, we read from Walt Whitman, Elizabeth Bishop, Etheridge Knight, Joy Harjo and others. But I want to help open whatever gates are possible into the group's most pressing experience and crucial perceptions, and I want to strip poetry of the institutional authority employed by countless bad teachers to unknowingly humiliate and alienate their classes. I think of the middle-aged woman in the post office at my university, who one day picked up a book of poems I received in the mail and, upon learning what it was, still opened it but asked, "Are these poems I can understand?" Whatever power poetry has, I think, must be for the students to grasp. It cannot be delivered by dictum or hearsay.

So I ask them to write narrative poems based on postcard images I bring in, and later they draw maps of their houses and neighborhoods, composing from the details they unearth here. The exercises migrate from the ostensibly impersonal to the intimate and back again, seeking to extend both territories. Sybil, Lee Ann and Teresa drift onto the subject of drinking. Teresa doesn't finish her poem. Instead, she is eager to tell me that she got drunk first at thirteen, with her father, and did a striptease for him with two other girls that evening. She then tries to retract the statement as her initial pride fades. Lee Ann recommends Advil and orange juice for hangovers. She, too, struggles with finishing her exercises but not because words elude her. She pours forth increasingly monumental monologues, sometimes captivating the group, especially the females. She bounces into an admirable impression of Lily Tomlin as Edith Ann. She declaims television ad copy and reproduces the chatter of emcees, pitch men, news commentators—becoming a parodic oracle mouthing the detritus of public expression, the most expensive phrases engineered. Part of her, I think, wants to *be* television, to possess its power to command attention. The daughter of a single mother who is a stockbroker, she offers tips on mutual funds and smart buys, all tinged with a sweet, manic loathing. Inside her notebook, which features Einstein on its cover, she has written in hundreds of lines the words "shut up!"

During one of her performances, Tommy, who is usually unable to focus on any task for more than a few minutes, bends unwaveringly over the postcard he has selected and the dictionary he has taken down from the shelf. I leave him alone, not wanting to stem what will be his longest period of work in my presence, hoping he will produce more than his usual ten to twenty slim lines. His poems invariably begin with "I am a...," as if each of his poignant, dashed-off compositions were another attempt at self-definition, a first level of naming he can't transcend.

While he labors, I think of the map he drew of his house, and his explanation of it.

"This is Dad's room, I'm not allowed to go in there. This is Grandma's room, I don't want to go in there because she smells. This is the porch, where I go if I'm allowed out."

Earlier, Sarah told me that Tommy's dad is, in fact, his gay uncle who "rescued him from the West Coast." Tommy's map was little more than a sketch, a cluster of blank squares. I encouraged him to elaborate, but he froze before the prospect.

Eventually, Tommy presents me with the piece that has so preoccupied him. No poem this time, but a rough translation of the caption on the back of a Russian postcard, which he has executed by replacing the Cyrillic letters with Arabic, aided by the dictionary. So smart, so truly beautiful, he possesses many of the qualities our culture rewards richly, yet his meteoric application, his constant fidgeting, cast his future in doubt. Were he considerably duller and plainer but steadier and driven toward advancement, there would be more places for him.

Laughter turns us toward the room at large. Sybil, Lee Ann and Teresa—sometimes buddies, just as often mortal foes—have put their hair in pigtails and are hamming it up. I capitalize on the moment, put all to work on poems about them. Lee Ann writes:

I like pigtails. They make me remember.
Remember what? Well, I never
wore pigtails as a child. I never
was a child. I was reading Forbes
magazine by the time I was 9.
A childhood is what I've always wanted.
So if I'm crazy like a kid, just
take it in stride. Accept it. I enjoy
acting like a 3-year-old. Pigtails
are not part of me. They are me, free,
flowing and sometimes hard to tame...

Sammy, a cute, wispy boy on whom Sybil has a crush this week, writes a rap about pigtails, which he belts out, and the room roars. At this moment, R.J. rumbles from the bathroom. Immense, stereotypically doltish, he can be violent, Sarah tells me, but I have only seen the gentle side, his pathetic confusion once when he sniffed his armpits not quite furtively after he had been teased by the girls about smelling bad. He calls me "sir," and says about his compositions such things as, "this doesn't suck too much, does it?" The map of his house and neighborhood is a lattice-work of thick, layered walls, perhaps as invisible to anyone else as the myriad emotional walls in this classroom. In two weeks, he will be removed from the program suddenly, his foster father collecting his articles, placing them in the car and then telling R.J., "You, you can walk home." But now R.J. lumbers into the middle of the class, into the spotlight of attention, grinning triumphantly, his hair rubber-banded into three prongs. The group erupts gleefully, and soon all the boys with hair enough are wearing multiple pigtails.

A month later I hear, in passing, from one of the administrators that a group performance has been scheduled. Perhaps it has been on the calendar since before my arrival, but the sidelong quality of the announcement makes me wonder why anyone thinks a public reading by these students is possible. The sessions in the previous weeks have grown more chaotic, reflecting a partial decline in the power of the point system to encourage compliance and an increasing strictness at the group homes, where chores have assumed a boot-camp magnitude. Lee Ann has tried to smuggle marijuana into the girls' home, inside a teddy bear. She has run away with Sammy, and both have returned after ten days, Lee Ann slightly droopy from medication, Sammy still clinging to his repugnant "gangsta" persona. Becky, who still labors to read her writing aloud, is back also, having been committed to the local psychiatric unit for depression and suicidal inclinations.

Anger tinges the insistent calm of the mauve walls, and its colors stain the atmosphere suddenly, repeatedly—a kicked desk, a thrown book, an uprising of insults. The seduction of "acting out" gathers momentum, and Sarah divides the room, drawing boundaries like an imperial arbiter. One of the administrators tells her that all the talk of suicide is just a form of manipulation, though she *should* respond to it. The kids seem black-eyed with exhaustion and an unwilling resignation. "They've taken all my points," says Teresa, "and how many more dishes can I wash?" I look on the board which displays the total points earned by each student. Level 7 is the top. Two students hover at Level 4, two at Level 2. The rest lie at Level 1.

More than before, I confront the emotional tone of the group and improvise, fashioning individual assignments on the spot with those willing to work. In this, I'm like that man on the old *Ed*

Sullivan Show, who kept a dinner plate spinning on each of a long row of flexible poles, dashing up and down the row, swirling now this pole, now that one, hoping to keep the whole shebang spinning. And there are crashes. One day I shout at the class to force its attention into some kind of consensus. At the break, Sarah asks me how I am, a little nervous about my having yelled. I tell her that I'm probably just tired. "Doesn't it get to be a bit much?" I say, "Doesn't it take more than it gives back?"

"I get money," she says softly, flatly. And I think of the wife of one of my colleagues, who admired me for my work with troubled youth, until she learned that I was being paid, though modestly. Somehow, that fact shifted my labor into another realm and reduced its worth—probably because, in this culture, most artists are expected to adore their calling so much that they are grateful to offer it any time free of charge, while a few of their number generate vast wealth, and concomitant awe, by inventing mass entertainments.

Still, in each class session, small rewards offer themselves. Sammy smiles slightly when I compliment him on one of his lines. Each time I arrive, Jed greets me at the door and asks to borrow my pen, and I always give it to him, though it is not my beloved fountain pen, which I leave in my car. More than once I witness a light in a face, a flicker of recognition and pleasure in being a maker, and my eyes water with the sentimentality of a childless man. Those who continue to write believe in words as action with an almost fundamentalist zeal. Like some of my more passionate students at the university—students often neglected and abused by busy, well-to-do parents—they sense how many forces have conspired to cut out their tongues, and they hunger, however remotely, for the power of intelligent articulation, the grace and intricate fury of words arranged like a feast to honor that which is humanly true. And this drive fosters a range of dangers, absurdities, triumphs. R.J., for instance, asks me how to write a love poem, because he is swooning with a crush on Sybil, encouraged by Lee Ann who knows that R.J.'s longing, if expressed, will result in his humiliation. Later I find his attempts abandoned, mercifully, to the wastebasket. At the conclusion of a brawl between Tommy and Becky, which Bob breaks up, there is a sudden, vast silence and Jed declares, as if having an epiphany, "This calls for a poem!" and plunges into writing. At last, Becky breaks through:

Walking Boys

You see Tommy talking, being
by Sammy, following Sammy,
copying Sammy. Tommy, you
get on people's nerves. You
try to show off at the computers,
in your school books. And how
you piss people off.

You see Jed talking, yelling,
shouting. Jed sits and tries
to get you in trouble. Some times
he acts out and does stuff and
blames it on other people.
Then he kisses butt. Jed,
you need to get a life.

You see Harry wearing cross
colors trying to be like this
kid that was kicked out. Harry,
before that kid came you were
nice, fun to be around. And
treated everyone . . . well, almost
everyone . . . with respect. Stop
trying to be like that kid. Just
be yourself.

For a while, I withhold from the students news of the performance, seeking to maximize its impact, since attention spans are
often short and the attraction of newness ephemeral. I browse
through my file of their poems, deciding which I will "suggest"
that each read, uneasy at the notion of a show which is supposed
to give them a "positive experience" while providing good publicity
for the organization. During a class break, one of the administrators
appears and discusses with Sarah the need to transfer Becky to
a facility with more supervision, but neither she nor Sarah have
reviewed Becky's file because it has vanished in the labyrinth of
social service offices. Acronyms pass between them, part of the
language of agency-world, with its metaphysics of concrete goals,
incremental achievement, measurable processes. Over and over,
the students are, to me, amorphous, and this quality, for better or
worse, collides with the hard surfaces of method. They are being
dealt with, even if they do not, or cannot, fit their spirits to the
system—which makes me wonder how much my file really differs
from the one lost.

One day I arrive to find the blinds drawn on the classroom—a strategy, I later learn, imposed by an administrator to sedate the group by reducing outside stimulation. When I announce the performance, most of the class remains impassive, rumor of it having already visited them. Others seem stricken with delight, or terror. All are accustomed to reading aloud, but for many the prospect of their words striking the public air transforms the room from an everyday prisonhouse into an exceptional haven. For the first time they recognize the security in their intimacy with their classmates, however painful. I pull up one of the blinds and point to the jacarandas across the street, which now rain their purple blossoms on a battered, gray Mazda parked at the curb. "That's poetry," I say, hoping to encourage them, "the blossoms and the heap." Teresa rolls her eyes and a derisive giggle or two percolates from the group, and we are underway again.

The evening before the performance—which will be part of a volunteer recognition dinner—we hold a rehearsal picnic at the boys' group home. An old, well-kept dwelling spawned by visions of large middle-class families residing in ample rooms, its gables project over the live oaks in the backyard. The sight of the kids in these comfortable surroundings seems incongruous, almost inappropriate, but I remind myself that this *is* where they live, the males, at least. The students and the half-dozen adults on hand sit quietly at the tables, or banter, or take a second burger off the grill, and the ordinariness of it all both shocks and reassures me. In recent months the class has been tutored by a dancer also, so it has been decided that the group will read its poems—all on the theme of "my neighborhood"—while enacting a series of choreographed moves. In the driveway, the kids practice their routines, some slightly gymnastic. Paul, the choreographer, has arranged the work so that at various points each of the participants will drift into the foreground of the stage and read a poem. He believes the body contains its emotional history, and movement can retrieve and express it. He knows also the emotional demands required of one who must hold another, or trust others enough to be held, and he has created a piece that encourages the group to confront itself as never before. Thus, the kids will measure a frontier with the various weights and pressures of their words *and* bodies.

They tumble, they squabble, practicing in small groups. Jed takes Sybil's hand, tentatively, to execute a turn; her touch is offered like a dark, velvet bag into which he reaches. Becky performs her slow flip aided by Tommy and Teresa, tossing herself backward, turning the world upside down again and again with greater confidence. Even one of the sideliners, Bill, decides he wants to be in the show, though he has written no poem, and Paul devises a place for him. I chew on the tip of my pen as everybody tries to meet their cues, mum so as not to further complicate the instructions. When we adjourn, at last, for Teresa's birthday celebration, they have walked through the entire program once, a halting jag about which they seem generally elated. The administrator on hand, the woman who had ordered the blinds drawn, appears grateful for their solidarity and bewildered about how to transport it to the school. Teresa grins over her cake. "C'mon, hurry up. Cut it," says the woman who oversees the girls' group residence, "because you all got to get home and have community time."

The next morning at our usual session, I have the kids rehearse the program once more, but they seem to have forgotten most of their cues, even the order of their readings. Lee Ann leads the disintegration, reconfiguring it into her brand of improvisational nonsense. Jed fumes at what he perceives as limitless irresponsibility. Tommy decides that he will probably make a mistake during the performance and so must withdraw. Everyone seems to be locking themselves in the bathroom and kicking chairs. Yet that evening, they are all veiled in an immense propriety around their dinner tables abutting the stage. Always, they lust for attention, but the kind they will receive tonight—so different from the usual therapeutic regard, or the glare and thump of trouble—cows them. Also, their performance is already underway: each starring as his or her best-behaved self. Again, their game faces remind me how much I project onto them my desire for them to be "normal," conventional—generalizing to that end repeatedly from even their smallest gestures.

I introduce them to my wife, about whom the girls are especially inquisitive. A hundred or so guests arrive, and we eat dinner and hear a few speakers and many thanks, and then it is time. The room darkens. Into a wan spotlight on the stage, Teresa steps sheepishly, perfectly, and begins to recite, "If you walked down my street, you'd hear a cat crying for food. . . ." Most of the kids have not memorized their poems, so they will read them from a typescript. I've made several photocopies of each for the group, especially Tommy, whom Bob has convinced to stay with the program and who has kept trying to sabotage himself by misplacing his copies.

Other spotlights pool on the stage, and several small groups mill with a haunting slowness. Somehow they are transformed by the moment. They are clumsy, bored teens on a street corner of the heart, children fallen from a jungle gym composed of human bodies. Their faces tilt downward, lift wearily to the spotlight as though to receive admonishment from the gods of all that is older and more powerful.

I look out across the audience—an appreciative assembly of volunteers, who know these kids well—and yet I wonder what they hear in these poems. There is in such public presentations an unspoken demand for adequate—*moving*—content. We want these young people to write about their broken homes and wretched parents—their slings and arrows—poignantly, so that we can be moved by their trials and perhaps glean satisfaction at what help we've offered them. Any furious pride and rebellious dignity they might possess, any ferocity they might direct toward us is not allowed. Anger of this sort is rarely recognized as art. There are acceptable confrontations and others which are dismissed as bad manners, rant, or cant.

The program continues, unbelievably, adding one small triumph to another. Becky reads for the first time without stumbling on her words. Delicately, with the restraint of one who has almost forsaken explaining, Sybil delivers her poem in which a love "potion" becomes a "poison." Jed lumbers forth, thumbs in his front pockets, a wizened man in a boy's body. The group shifts like a smoky constellation. It jumps and shouts. It leans and stands, a larger unity. And then—partly to show off, partly in genuine goodwill—Lee Ann, the last reader, offers an elegant impromptu thank-you speech on behalf of her classmates, and the show is over.

As the group bows to the generous applause, I wonder about the people beyond this audience—citizens in a culture where pain is quickly sentimentalized, where the suffering of one person is witnessed by millions through media that divorces witnessing from feeling. What would they hear in the words of these children? No doubt it is easy to forget how much these kids are responsible for the current state of their lives. In my months around the group school I have seen parents frightened and confused by their children, as well as parents brutish and criminal. But in a time of government downsizing, where "personal responsibility" is becoming the newest device to relieve us of the reality that we live with others, shouldn't we also ask: How responsible can a

Donald Morrill

child be? If he can't learn responsibility from his parents, if she can't learn to care for herself from them, where will he or she learn if the doors beyond family are shut by a callous society?

Poetry won't save these kids, if it is that kind of saving they need. Still, they recognize that it offers a form of salvation in a culture itself starving for poetry as it accepts weak substitutes and tries to destroy the poetic spirit. Various believers in their voices, these kids will need their belief in order to be heard, to make a better way, even by themselves. Of them all, I think most often of Tommy. During that vital performance he didn't sabotage himself, and later he had to admit to his success, an admission he found exceptionally difficult. In the spotlight, among his classmates, he had read his poem with a sad clear song in his throat, unhurried, his free hand hanging motionless, for once, at his side:

I am a rose
my stem is
strong I am
In a field
of daisies
I have
strong roots
I have to
fight for
water my
spirit is
strong I
have delicate
petals I
will always
be the one
strong flower
I am

Donald Morrill is our Editors' Prize winner in the essay. His work has appeared widely, and he is the author of a memoir entitled *A Stranger's Neighborhood*.

CAPTAINS BY DEFAULT / *Scott Boylston*

T HE SNOW IS DELICATE and knee high. It is cotton candy in my mouth, too fleeting to satisfy but enjoyable just the same. I bend in mid stride and shovel the powder with my gloved hand. With this motion I leave a smooth and straight gully that strikes me as the most perfect consequence of my effort, conspicuous in its complete lack of fault. I pack the snow against the roof of my mouth and suck it of its moisture. The remains trickle down my throat.

We trudge over the white curves of the golf course with tempered anticipation, led by Brad. His shin pads thrust forward and spoil the chaste evenness of the snow as clots of it roll across the surface with each footstep. Brad is like his father, neither tall nor short. His broad shoulders buttress a head of dirty blond hair and keen eyes. The eyes are steadily indifferent, the hair as straight as his stance. When we play dibble in the lake, the stick is most often found in Brad's grasp.

Behind him, Tim concentrates with narrow diligence on the impressions left by Brad. He is smaller than Brad in every way. He walks with his head down and his eyes rapt on the heels in front of him. His is the pursuit of a disciple, convinced of salvation through emulation. He follows Brad this way through grass and mud as well as snow.

The pond is a smudge in the distance. It borders a brief but dense wood that stands like an oasis upon the sculpted rolls of the course. It is a rectangular basin with steep, powder-packed banks that serve us well as backboards. On the far corner is a pump that runs year-round, in a small wooden shed, isolated on its perch. On one side it is braced by a thicket of evergreen and on the other side by the tar-black water it refuses to let freeze. Its influence reaches ten feet in each direction, the resulting hole the only blemish on the otherwise smooth ice. There is no desire within our group to explore the monotonous groans and darkened windows of the pump house or the lightless hole it creates in the ice. It is never mentioned between us.

I am third in line. I follow without thought of being led. The terrain of the golf course is as familiar to me as the musty crawl space that extends from the cellar of my house. I recognize slouching firs that have sheltered trenched and tunneled forts stocked with snowball grenades and icicle rations, sand traps that have served as bunkers in warmer weather, and broad oaks and maples that still hold skeletal remains of meticulously built tree forts attended to more during their construction than any time after. This familiarity has not tarnished my intrigue, but allowed it to prosper.

Stan and Ian Finch walk in unison behind me. They are often mistaken for twins. The actual discrepancy in their age is secreted by their equal eagerness to please, just as a retriever and her grown pup can appear to be from the same litter. They are not bothered by this, not even Stan, the elder of the two, but relish the low profile and anonymity of sharing an identity. Halloween finds them draped in matching white sheets. They have eye holes and slits for their mouths that are smeared with chocolate and spit. They have been ghosts for several years and have no complaints.

Each winter we vow to recover the countless pucks that slap into the inky water like skipping stones before finally nose diving, or skid to the brink at a taunting crawl only to slip over the edge just at the moment we thought they would stop. We joke that soon an island of black rubber will rise from the murky water like a volcano, and we will make a fortune selling the black disks by the truckload. But by spring's resurgence we have other crusades in mind.

We each bring two pucks—the oldest ones we can find—pocked with misuse on summer-heated asphalt. If luck accompanies us out, and we do not lose all of our pucks, we play until the scarcity of light assigns all objects the same color, then we reluctantly retrace our path in the moonglow. We are careful not to pass too close to the wooded areas where shadows from creaking branches hang like webs on the blue surface of the snow. We still harbor the fears of childhood. The journey back may take minutes or hours, interrupted by tussles or snow angel exhibitions or lying on our backs watching our own huffs of breath against a velvet sky. We are each the last soul on earth. We move only with regret, urged by a tingling of our backsides and the inevitable tickling itch growing around our feet that will stay with us long after the warmth of home has chased away the cold from our bodies.

Virgil trails the pack by several yards. If not for his sheer inability to brave the untrod snow without quickly losing pace, he would set his own course. He is stronger in mind than in body. His insistence that the pond can be reached more quickly by first walking farther north on the road rather than trekking directly across the contours of the blanketed course falls on deaf ears. We cross this way because the rest of us agree with Brad when he says it is more fun to create your own trail. Virgil's disinclination is worn on his face and posture. He drags his equipment behind him, like a dog on a leash, through the snow. Virgil's opinions, no matter how vehemently conveyed, encourage scorn from Brad and wary disregard from the rest of us. He is mouse-like with a red nose that runs with things better left unseen. His hair is matted as if he has just taken off a baseball cap for the first time in weeks. His appearance is irksome. His demeanor, in response to our continuous dismissal, has grown to match his appearance.

Virgil refuses to shoulder his equipment-clad hockey stick, and his stakes occasionally clank in protest. He breathes heavily, martyred. We weave through the concealed hazards of the golf course behind Brad like a row of railway cars. We cross the open spaces as soldiers on the march, fully armed, our weapons slung cocksure over our shoulders. Our feet squeak in near unison on the snow. We are Washington's men at Valley Forge, Napoleon's troops before Waterloo, Snow White's six dwarves with Grumpy at the rear rubbing his runny nose and dragging his shovel all the way. The brittle cold air brings sharp sensation into our lungs and pinches our nostrils. Stillness whistles past, and we breathe like dragons.

When we reach the pond we sit on our jackets and lace up. The jackets remain as rest stops and penalty seats. We dress in our heroes' jerseys and rarely match our teammates. Stan and Ian are the exception. There are no goalies, no defensemen, no left wings, right wings or centers; there are only hockey players. We shoot for the space between our opponents' discarded boots. Over the bank is over the crossbar. To compensate for the dark pool of unfrozen water, we swing our boots toward the opposite corner.

We rarely lose a puck to the snow that surrounds the pond, and we never moan when one breaches the shallow crest. Instead there is a hysterical rush to the hidden puck and whoever recovers it is rewarded with a goal. We charge the bank, glide for a step and then, with eyes wide, we leap, knees or head first, diving into the snow and digging like mad. There are days when a thin and fragile layer of ice coats the snow and the puck leaves a telltale hole where it lands. These frenzied quests provide us with a tension breaker from our game, which we play with the violence if not the skill or talent of our idols. Tempers flare, and with them gloves and sticks fly.

I am captain by default. Tim will not willingly oppose Brad who, again by default, albeit one of a different nature, is captain of the other side. Stan and Ian refuse to step forward. Virgil is pushed back whenever he tries. I am fortified by the Finch brothers, invariably a package deal. Virgil is teamed with Brad and Tim. We play the best of five games and win because Virgil is ignored by his teammates.

We do not have periods but break on mutual exhaustion. Snow provides nourishment. We take it in slowly, wary of the dull ache that too much cold at one time will invite. We wipe past the top layers and dig into virgin snow and bring the precious mound to our faces slowly so that none of the powder is lost. We lap at it with the hope that just once we will get more than we already know we will get. It feels good to lie still and we lob snow at each other in lazy arcs, laughing and coughing up the cold air.

Our game starts up again slowly with the more eager rising to skate in shiftless circles with a puck or ice chunk bouncing between the wooden blades of their sticks. We shuffle teammates so that I have Virgil and Tim and the Finch brothers are with Brad. It is ancient law that Brad and I never side on the same team. It goes unsaid and unquestioned.

With the new alignment Tim passes indiscriminately, as if Virgil has just stepped onto the ice. There is no sign of the scorn so venomously exhibited in the first games. Without Brad's influence, Virgil becomes a competent teammate in Tim's eyes. In fact, Virgil and Tim share a certain tenacity, as well as an unspoken appreciation for each other's manic drive to prove themselves. They are more like each other than either knows, or would admit. We lose ourselves in the game, breathing heavily and finding that our lungs expand in compensation. There is a freshness at the bottom of them.

Tim passes the puck in my direction, but Brad, sensing Tim's intentions, cuts between the two of us and skates at full speed toward our goal. Only Virgil is between Brad and the net, and he skates backward watching Brad's eyes. He is awkward but firm in his motion. Brad is capable of quickly getting the puck past Virgil, his wrist shot is hard and sure, but instead he thrusts forward and engages Virgil. There is a collision, but not of the sort we expect. Virgil is not flattened. Instead, the blade of his stick deftly slaps the puck away and then inadvertently slips between the stanchions of Brad's skates. Brad falls immediately onto his stomach and slides toward the snowbank. The brunt of the impact is absorbed by his head. There is a faint crunch and then silence as the rest of us skate to a halt.

The brief hush is shattered by mirth at the sight of Brad as he turns his head, nostrils packed with snow. The force of the blow has driven both his eyelids upward, and we wears a dazed smile. He blows a snow pellet from a nostril and we laugh again. Brad is unaccustomed to this side of mockery. There is another short silence as he unsteadily rises to his skates and shakes his head free of snow, nearly losing his balance. This is too much for us. Tim slips and falls to the ice he is laughing so hard. Stan and Ian fall into a snowbank. Virgil smiles meekly and allows his body to sag in amusement.

We all look away from Brad momentarily, and so no one sees him rush headlong toward Virgil. Before anyone knows what is happening he buries his shoulder into Virgil's chest. We watch him fall to the ice and curl up in pain, the breath knocked out of him. Brad skates back to where his stick has fallen and swoops to pick it up without stopping. There is no sound other than the methodical ripping of Brad's blades on the ice he skates back toward Virgil. He wears a dubious grin we have all seen, not knowing if it reflects leniency or retribution. He glides to Virgil, who is still trying to get his breath, and hooks the blade of his stick between one of his skates. He circles him slowly so that Virgil spins on his back like a top. This apparently benign retort settles the rest of us and we chuckle at the sight. Virgil also relaxes somewhat and plays along.

After several turns Brad straightens his line and tows Virgil around the pond. He turns and then turns again so that the two of them make a figure eight. We applaud the performance. The relief and appreciation of being a part of something shows on Virgil's face. He has almost forgotten the pain in his chest. They are a figure skating team. Brad goes into a tight spin and Virgil revolves around him like a satellite. there are cheers from the rest of us. Brad again breaks out of the formation and then skates to the corner furthest from the pumphouse and its dark moat. He pauses in the corner as if preparing to make his final pass. Brad takes a bow, careful to keep his stick high enough to prevent Virgil from freeing his foot. Uncertainty fills my stomach like syrup. Brad throws a complicit glance toward Tim, whose face quickly drains of amusement. He rises and skates toward the two and smiles with a plea. No words pass between anyone, as if we all know our roles. Brad nods toward Virgil's other skate. Tim obeys his unspoken command and hooks Virgil's free skate with his own stick. We titter as if to assure Brad that he need not take the threat any further, he is in control once again. He tips his head toward the quivering water and looks into Timås eyes.

They are forty feet away from the unfrozen area and picking up speed. Brad and Tim are on either side of Virgil, who is spread-eagled between them like the contents of a slingshot. The last hint of uneasy laughter is swallowed by the sound of steel edges cutting ice. Stan and Ian look at each other and then down to their feet. I stand when they are twenty feet away. I hope the motion along will distract them and bring them back. Of course, it does not. Tim has abandoned his glances toward Brad and is staring vacantly in obedience.

I skate into their path and yell Brad's name, but I am not there for him. The frigid pool is behind me; I am at its edge. I hear the hum of the pump, and the patient lapping of the water. I take two strides and jump at Brad. My shoulder hits him in the stomach and he leaves his feet as I push him down to the ice with a resounding crack. I think to myself that it is a good hit. I land on top of him. In one motion he rolls on top of me, punches me in the face and stands, but he is hurt. He holds his gut and bends over in pain. He skates away, laughing under his breath.

Tim, still holding Virgil by the skate, comes to a stop two feet from the edge of the ice. There is guilt about him, then quick anger, like I spoiled his fun. He skates by and mutters an obscenity as I lie on the ice with blood dripping from my nose. He follows Brad to their boots and begins unlacing his skates. Brad already has his skates off and is bending over in pain. He continues laughing as both of them walk off the ice and into the barren landscape. They follow the same course that led them here. Brad walks in our footprints and Tim pushes through untread snow directly beside him. I look back at Virgil, but he watches each one of us without expression. We are accomplices, witnesses, one no better than the other. Our silence is our guilt. Ian's eyes have not left the ground, Stan's have not left the darkening sky. I focus my attention on the stiff blood on my skin and how the caked substance cracks when I wiggle my upper lip. The air is new within my nostrils.

The Finch brothers rise and skate slowly to their boots. Not a word is spoken as they dress for the journey home. They do not look in our direction but instead throw glances at the receding figures of Brad and Tim. Then they are up and off with a feeble acknowledgment. They walk at a slow and deliberate pace to the path and then speed up in random spurts. They run for several strides and then slow back down, almost in unison. As they move further from the pond the sprints come more frequently until they are almost galloping through the snow, plowing ahead like dogs after their master.

I come very close to laughing at the sight of Virgil. His nose is as red as I've ever seen it. He follows the progression of the Finch brothers with narrow eyes, and then lifts himself and skates past me. I think he does not realize I am there as his skate blade comes within inches of my bare hand. I know I will not move until he leaves or says something. I have no desire to speak a word to him, and I dread to hear his voice. I watch dark ripples make their way across the flat water and bump harmlessly into the stark whiteness of ice. The pump is like a heartbeat; it drones despite the cold, despite everything. I feel as if the island of black rubber is about to emerge, as dark and still and cold as the water that conceals it. I pay no attention as Virgil makes his way across the golf course. He does not follow the others, but cuts directly across toward the road somewhere off through the trees. His progress is slow, and laborious, and irrefutable. He becomes a dot in the distance like the rest of them.

I stand and skate toward the snow bank that holds my belongings. I sit, remove my skates and rub the sleepy tingle from my feet. It is a wonderful feeling. The sun is nearly absent. It seeps through dark trees on the horizon. I walk home over untrod snow, and go out of my way to avoid our old trails. As the last glow of sun thins to purple I fall into the snow and lie still and listen to the empty creaking of winter.

This is **Scott Boylston's** first publication.

Scott Boylston

SERENISSIMA / *Paula Huston*

T HEY HAD LITERALLY BEEN planning this trip for years—
Shana had longed to see Italy since she was a girl—and
they were supposed to have gone in 1952, for their honeymoon.
But they'd had no money at all and the war devastation still
lay across Europe like a smoking blanket and so it was put off,
though with the absolute promise to one another that they'd go
as soon as they possibly could—certainly before they had a child.
However, Amy, unplanned and unexpected, was born less than
a year later, and the trip was of course out of the question while
she was still toddling about. Besides, Perry had just started his
new job with Boeing, and how could they think about giving up
the money when other young couples they knew were struggling
so?

Then, in 1955, Shana's grandmother died and left them enough
cash to either buy a house or travel to Europe. They'd actually
bought liner tickets for the summer when Shana found she was
pregnant again. They postponed the voyage, thinking they'd go
the following year, but Chris's birth was not easy, and then
Shana's sister lost her infant to some mysterious ailment that
struck him down in the crib, and suddenly Shana slipped into
a sorrow so profound that she had to be hospitalized for three
months. The doctors called it "postpartum depression"; all Shana
knew was that night after night she could not sleep, no matter
how exhausted she was or how her eyes burned, and that often
she would find her face wet with tears she was not even aware
of shedding. Eventually she recovered, but in the same way, she
thought, that one recovers from a knee injury; scar tissue had
formed and the apparatus of her psyche was looser, more fragile.
Where she'd once characterized herself as brave and hopeful, she
now often felt shadowed by a free-floating fear that she had to
work hard to hide. This time when the trip was postponed, it
was put off indefinitely; her grandmother's money went into a
three-bedroom house in a clean, modest neighborhood, and Perry
and Shana settled down, as best they could, to the raising of
their family.

But now it was 1970, the girls were seventeen and fifteen, and
they were finally making the trip together. It was the middle

of July, a steamy Italian summer afternoon, and they had been driving for hours through thick, polluted heat on their way to one of the world's greatest cities. Shana was staring out the window, searching for Venice amidst the factory haze and shipyard confusion that surrounded it, when she spotted the sign, "Serenissima," the campground they'd been seeking. It was just off the main highway to Padua and along a dirty canal, but well back from the road at least. An old villa, typically Italian, with its plaster peeling back from its rose-colored bricks and a long tree-lined lane behind it with tents scattered about on the grass. As they turned in at the gate, the girls began to stir and waken, grumpy from their long, heated naps.

"Shana, how much does the book say?" Perry asked her.

"Fourteen thousand lire."

"Not bad for this close to the city. Look, there's even a bus stop."

By now they had been married for eighteen years, they'd been through some difficult times together (she thought, in an awful flash, of her months in the hospital) but Perry had never lost his capacity for delight. Look! There's a bus stop! She knew that they did not see the world in the same way. He had the slight energetic body of a boy, the thick curling hair and hornrimmed glasses of a scholar, and the soul, she sometimes told him, of a saint to have put up with the dubious, flinching nature she'd developed in the years after her breakdown. She'd cultivated a habit of always holding something back, a practice she despised in others and knew to be cowardly in herself even while she clung to it year after year, her supposed shield against future grief. Even her girls—she loved them deeply, but with a certain wariness.

But now they were in Italy, they'd found their campground, they were only a few short miles from Venice, and together they would finally see a sight they'd worked toward nearly all their married life: the dark, serpentine canals, the rainbow of gondolas on the water, the mountainous cathedral of San Marco rising up in all its Byzantine splendor through clouds of sunstruck pigeons.... She turned toward her husband, wanting to say something loving and grateful to commemorate the occasion, something like *he* might say if only he'd thought of it first, but they were already parked beside the camp office and a compact young man had come to Perry's window and was asking for their passports. After a week in Italy Shana was used to this procedure, though she still felt

Paula Huston

violated by it. How did they know they would ever get their documents back? They could be sold or lost...but today, in her anticipatory Venice mood, she didn't mind so much. The young man, all business, murmured "grazie" as he shuffled through their papers; she noticed his lush, greased pompadour, his gold cross, his sleeveless undershirt, tucked neatly into gray business pants, and was convinced that such a responsible-looking person would have a family of his own—that he understood their situation, the vulnerability of an American family on the road, and would not let them down.

After they'd checked in, Perry drove them through the campground until they found a cool site in long grass under two trees. Amy and Chris, hot and irritable as they were, helped their father set up the tents while she unpacked the food box. Then, finished with their chores, the girls went in search of ice-cream bars; she sat down on the warm grass, watching them as they strolled off down the road in their long-legged nonchalant teenaged beauty. The heat shimmered around them, turning them into peasant girls walking a dusty lane in a Van Gogh landscape; the cicadas ground away above them like dry bones rattling, and the leaves of the trees that shadowed them were dark green and monstrous, like rainforest leaves.

When she was their age, she'd yearned with an unrelenting, smokey-eyed passion for Italy and had never been able to see it. Now these daughters of hers, who had very likely never given Venice a thought, were here in the place of that long-dead dreamer, her girlhood self—and she was glad, of course, but also feeling something closer to sorrow than to the unmitigated joy she'd expected. Was it regret? Perhaps. It would make an odd kind of sense. For she was just beginning to realize she could no longer experience Italy as she once might have. It was too late, too much had happened to her. She could appreciate the architecture and the fabulous artwork, but the haunting passion was gone, along with her youth and her courage.

Perry, checking the oil in their rented car, was smiling at her from under the open hood. "Serenissima," he said. "Only in Italy could you find a campground with a name like that."

She nodded absently, still caught up in the image of herself at seventeen—herself, and the longing to do, to see, to travel that for so many years, at least until the breakdown, had translated itself into hope and good cheer. Who had that person been? How had she vanished so completely?

He turned his head. "Did you hear that?" he said, and suddenly she became aware of the sound of crying, a thin, wavering, doglike sound coming from close by. They waited. The crying went on for another minute at least, and then stopped abruptly, as though cut off. "Where are the girls?" he asked her.

"Ice cream."

He went back to the engine. She listened for a moment longer, but the crying, which had made her shiver, was over. She got to her feet slowly because of the heat, and went to the tent where she gathered up her towel and washcloth, fresh underwear, deodorant. She was sticky from the long ride and from the effort of setting up camp; it was time for a shower. Amy and Chris would want showers too before they all had dinner and caught the bus into Venice for the evening. The girls liked to cook and usually made the evening meal, but today, to save time, she'd shower first, then get dinner ready before they returned from their lazy exploration of the old estate. She climbed out of the tent with her supplies wrapped in the towel and walked down the lane in the direction the girls had gone, thinking she remembered seeing the restroom off to the left.

Yes, there it was—she turned up a row of blue tents and passed beside an empty, soot-smeared bus with writing on it that she couldn't read. Not a soul anywhere; everyone must be in the city. Good—she'd have the showers to herself. She started through the door, humming, just as the young man from the campground office came bursting out. She stopped, embarrassed; he, panting and pale, raised his hands to hold her at the entrance. "No," he said in his broken English. "It is impossible."

"Impossible?"

"You do not understand," he said. "A woman...." He put his hands around his neck, squeezed, made the sign of a rope hanging from a beam.

"Oh my God," she said, suddenly dizzy. "You're *kidding*."

He, however, was nodding vigorously, and a sweet-faced blonde woman she hadn't noticed before stepped out from behind him, nodding also.

"Somebody hung herself?"

"Yes," he said solemnly, and she thought he might cry. Her eyes leaped automatically to the interior of the room behind him and she jerked them away before they could adjust to the darkness. The blonde woman was staring at her dazedly, as though she expected something. Comfort, perhaps? Advice? Shana thought of Chris and Amy, their careless stroll down the lane on a Van Gogh afternoon, and how easily they might have been the ones to stumble in on this instead of the blonde woman, who was by now looking as though she needed to sit down and hang her head between her knees. Shana went to put an arm around her shoulders. The woman heaved four great sighs, passed her hand over her eyes, shook for a moment, then gave Shana a rueful smile, as though she'd committed some unforgivable rudeness in public. "Would you like to sit down?" Shana asked her. She shrugged; it was clear she did not speak a word of English.

The young man attempted to take charge of the situation. Other women, he made them understand, would be arriving at the restroom soon, unaware of what had happened; they must prevent a scene. Together the three of them dragged two trashcans in front of the door while Shana's mind went to the thin, doglike sound of crying, so abruptly cut off, and a single phrase, repeated over and over again: Five minutes earlier and I would have been the one to find her. She felt meek and disoriented, like someone with a head injury.

The young man asked them to stay by the doorway while he went to call the carabinieri. The two women huddled close together, united by the thing that dangled a few feet away. Shana wondered what nationality her blonde companion was—perhaps a Czech with her high cheekbones and broad white face. She seemed all right now; the danger of fainting seemed past. She's probably seen worse, Shana thought, just as an apparition of the dead woman materialized before her mind's eye. The woman was youngish—thirty-two or three perhaps—with dark hair in a braid down her back and three children at home. She was wearing a cotton skirt, too long, and sandals, one of which had fallen from her foot and lay beside the kicked-over chair. On this steamily hot day, she was also wearing, inexplicably, a red and blue sweater.

Shana closed her eyes for a moment and sagged against the restroom wall. The stranger had her face. How could it be? But for a moment she had seen it—her own face, closed, triumphant, swollen above the rope-bitten neck, believing it had conquered death.

And then the young man was back, bringing with him a heavy-set person in a Dutch fishing cap who was smoking a cigar. The two men squeezed sideways past the trashcans and went into the restroom. Shana heard a loud expletive in a language she didn't recognize, and suddenly the blonde woman began to cry fiercely, then rubbed her eyes just as fiercely and stopped. Well, that's it, then, Shana thought, striving for her usual distance but instead beginning to shiver. She's truly dead—and that man with the cigar must know her.

Other women, back from the day in Venice, were trickling into the area, milling around at the door. Nobody seemed to understand what was happening, why they couldn't use the bathroom. They murmured among themselves in various languages, looking inquiringly at Shana and the blonde woman. Amy and Chris wandered up and Shana rushed forward to stop them. "Something's happened," she said, her eyes suddenly filling with tears. "Something terrible. Go tell your father to come."

"What's going on?" Amy asked, craning to see.

"No," Shana said sharply. "Don't look in there. A woman...committed suicide."

"Oh my God," Amy said—and Shana recognized, in the midst of her daughter's obvious shock, clear signs of excitement, the way her eyes went instinctively to the dark interior beyond the open door. She's thinking *Wait until I tell my friends*, Shana thought. What in the world have I taught her? Chris, after an astonished look, stood somberly beside her sister. Chris was younger and more sensitive than Amy; Chris was like Perry. After her breakdown, Shana suddenly remembered, she had stopped holding Chris except to feed her. At the time it had seemed essential that she not touch the sweet skin or cuddle the warm baby weight in her lap unless she had to.

Shaken by the memory, she said, "Go back to camp. I'll be there in a minute, as soon as the police come." She had no idea why she was still standing by the doorway but it seemed her obligation to wait until the authorities arrived, and she was good at fulfilling her obligations. Oh yes, she thought, I'm good at that—and her eyes filled again at the thought of her daughters, especially Chris, standing beside the mouth of this open sepulchre.

The ambulance came first, an orange-and-white affair that pulled up beside the building in a flurry of gravel. Young men got out, drawing on clear plastic gloves. Shana pulled aside a trash can and they marched past her into the bathroom. A long moment of silence, then brash young men's voices speaking in Italian, and even a laugh, broken off. They have to be this way, she told herself. How could you see this kind of thing every day and not become hardened? She imagined the woman hanging inside—

the woman with *her* face—and the gentle, almost imperceptible corkscrewing of the body on its rope.

She was very tired all of a sudden, wanting nothing but a long nap, a blank sleep that would erase what had happened. I should get away from here, I should fix dinner, she thought, and just then Perry came up beside her and put his arm firmly around her shoulders. "What are you *doing* here?" he asked her, and she saw his eyes, too, go to the awful and mysterious place beyond the door. "Come on back to camp, Shana." She thought of arguing, but she was so very tired; she let him lead her down the road, even put her head on his shoulder for a moment.

"I heard she was Polish," said Amy excitedly. "From one of those big Polish tour buses—see all the blue tents down there? And the rest of the group is in Venice for the day and nobody knows yet but the bus driver—the guy with the cigar."

"How did you hear all this?" Shana asked her.

Amy shrugged. "Someone said she was a second-grade teacher."

"I need a beer," Shana said.

"I'll get you one," said Chris, and set off down the lane. Shana watched her head turn as she passed the restroom with the parked ambulance beside it.

They made dinner. Perry came up twice and kissed her, something she knew that he often wanted to do—a simple and affectionate gesture, consistent with his nature—but which he usually suppressed out of deference to her reserve. Tonight, however, not only did she appreciate it, but his sweetness made her want to cry. I have to let this go, she thought—all of this. She was terrified of crying; the first sign of tears, and she felt the shadow of the hospital, those terrible sleepless weeping nights, brooding over them all.

She stirred curry powder into a bowl of milk, purposely brisk, and licked her finger when it splashed on her hand. She thought of the young ambulance attendants, that brief, sharp, laughing expletive from inside the death chamber. Buck up, she told herself. You'll get through this.... She ran down the usual list of what she had: she was alive and in good health; her family was alive; that was all that mattered, really. The poor woman and her three children in Poland, waiting for their mother to come back.... But she couldn't think of her; she had her own family to think of. She looked with fierce possessiveness at their neat campsite, their three tents sitting in a row, their white rented car, her blue gas stove.

Then she heard the sirens. The whole campground looked up for a moment as two toylike vehicles with flashing lights pulled up in front of the restroom. The leaves on the trees trembled a bit at their passing, then stopped. Four carabinieri in dark blue pants with red stripes up the side pulled themselves from their tiny cars and strode in their black knee boots to the open door, where they stood for long moments talking. When they finally went inside, the ambulance attendants followed them. After a time one of the policemen emerged from the darkness and went to his car where he swung himself sideways in the seat, booted feet resting in the grass outside the open door, and said what needed to be said into the radio. Chris was coming back down the lane with Shana's beer just then, and Shana watched as her youngest passed by him—knew, without having to see it, exactly where and how the young man's deathshocked eyes found refuge in her daughter's lovely flesh.

Together she and Perry spread the red-and-white-checked table-cloth on the grass and the family proceeded, as best they could, to eat their dinner. An evening breeze came up, the air cooled off a bit, and Perry's yellow mosquito candle flickered in its bowl in the middle of the tablecloth. Shana sipped her beer and put forkfuls of curried rice into her mouth, chewing and swallowing dutifully in spite of her knotted stomach...and then the hearse arrived, a long blue police van with big back doors, like stage curtains. Inside rested a plastic coffin the color of the sky. A sigh—she could hear it like the ripple of hot wind through corn—passed over the campground. She thought of the blonde woman and hoped that someone (a daughter like Chris, perhaps) had given her a beer.

They could not finish their curry and rice after all. The girls stacked the dishes and Shana shook out the tablecloth, thinking that they really *had* to do some laundry soon, and then the coffin, carried by four officers and two ambulance attendants, came floating out the door. The men moved slowly, as though in a funeral procession, and everyone paused for a long moment to watch it as it went by. There goes death, Shana told herself, but the thought, when articulated that way, seemed to evaporate and lose its meaning. Death is impossible, she was thinking instead. It can't *be*. Yet she could remember clearly her sister's dazed and grieving face at the baby's funeral, and the way that she herself had to keep watch by Chris's crib night after night, never sleeping, until the moment her mind had cracked with utter weariness. She shuddered, picturing the dark inside of the coffin, the woman lying on her back with her hands folded across her stomach, hidden away from the random breeze that might set her turning. But, thought Shana, she's *safe* in there.

She began to weep for the first time in years, though not loudly, not obviously, not so her daughters could see. Why am I crying? she thought. I don't even know her...but it was not just the woman, it was all of them, every mortal one of them for whom she wept. How could it have been designed this way? She thought of Chris, Amy, Perry, her own little family, and how vulnerable they were. It made no sense. If we're supposed to love, she thought, then how can we be expected to give it up like this? Yet even as the tears came, she could feel the word struggling up out of her heart once again, defiant and insuppressible: *Safe*. And she knew then what Perry had perhaps been living with for years: that she was not yet out of the hospital.

They did not go into Venice that night. Shana drank more beer and sat up by candlelight trying to read. At ten, when it was time to brush teeth, shower, sleep, the girls came to her like the small children they'd once been and said they did not want to go into the reopened women's room alone and so she went with them, dreading it, and took both their hands in a way she could not remember doing before as they went together through the door.

The bathroom, lined on one side by white plaster shower stalls with dirty curtains and on the other by a row of Italian toilets (holes in the floor with footpads on which to crouch), was lighted by a single yellow bulb. A wooden chair stood at one end of the room beside the sink and mirror. The three of them, Shana and her two daughters, stood in the middle of the room, looking at the chair and at the beam above them. The sense of recent death, the dank piney smell of disinfectant, were so strong they almost knocked her over...but by morning, of course, with strong sunlight flooding in and new campers arriving, all casually unaware of what had happened only hours before their arrival at Serenissima, the aura of death was gone. And by the time she and her family pulled out that afternoon, they might have been, Shana thought, the last ones left in the campground who were there when it happened.

The young Italian man, wearing a crisp pink shirt, gave her a somber look as he handed back their passports; *he* wouldn't forget, nor would the blonde woman, but if he were the businessman he seemed, he'd never bring up the subject again, and the discovery of the Polish woman's body, perhaps the most traumatic moment of his life, would close over in his heart like the monstrous rainforest leaves of the campground trees had closed over her daughters strolling down the Van Gogh lane, gold with summer dust.

Nineteen-seventy ended; time went by. This trip was not the last Shana and Perry took, but it was the last with the whole family together. The girls had several more years of high school to get through, and then there was college to be paid for and the family savings account was drained for a time. She and Perry still traveled, but they took short trips to places in the United States, places they could afford. Their Italian adventure, their dream trip with all of its chapters and moments of crisis, became part of the family history, along with the boxes of slides, which were dragged out periodically for different boyfriends or for family gatherings. At those times it seemed odd to Shana that she could no longer remember the details of those three hard weeks on the road—that she could no longer conjure up the taste of the curry they ate almost every night, or the smell of the rain on the grass outside the tent. Things faded and blurred; even the girls, caught for single sunshot moments by the camera, looked like strangers in the pictures. Had they ever been so lanky, so coltish? Especially Chris?

Very rarely, she thought of the afternoon at Serenissima. She did not like to think of it, and pushed the scene away when it rose in her mind. So much had happened since that day; what was the point of thinking of it now? She'd changed for the better since then; she'd had to, with Chris and Perry to take care of. Serenissima had been the low point in a long journey that she suspected was not yet over, but at least she no longer brooded about death that way.

And so the intense and troubling memory, because she would not think of it, finally distilled itself down to a mere handful of images: the sweet face of the blonde woman who had discovered the body, her own arm around the woman's shoulders, those four deep sighs. Sometimes Shana also saw the blue coffin swaying past, or the wooden chair beside the sink and herself beneath the beam, a daughter clutching each of her hands. She could no longer remember the face of the young Italian man or even what Perry had looked like back then.

In 1994, however, twenty-four years after their original trip, she suddenly became obsessed with Venice. She was getting old; her childhood memories were becoming sharper and more poignant than almost everything that had followed them; miraculously, her girlhood longing for Italy was back in all its urgent splendor. First she called a travel agent, and then, breathless with excitement, she made the more difficult call to Amy, to ask for help with Perry. "But you're almost *seventy* Mom," Amy said. "How can you go alone?" Amy was a good daughter but she talked too much; Shana laughed at her, and then cried a little, hiding it, thinking of leaving Perry behind. "Oh, Mom," said Amy, contrite, "you *know* I'll take care of him. That's not the issue at all. We'll get the bed moved to my place and the nurse can come here every morning instead. That's not why I'm objecting. It's *you*— you're not that strong anymore. But don't listen to me; I worry too much...." Amy was forty-one now, almost as old as Shana had been during the first trip. And Amy had girls the same ages that she and Chris had been—it all seemed eerie to Shana, the great circle they had made.

The tragedy was Perry. She could hardly bear to tell him she was leaving, but if she waited...? Who knew how many more years he would linger in a memoryless wasteland, this shadow-haunted landscape he'd occupied for almost a decade already? She'd watched his muscles wither, his frame shrink; she'd watched him slowly curl down into himself like a dying plant. Now, when they walked, she pushed him in his wheelchair under a blanket while his head bobbed like a baby's and his wandering eyes struggled to focus on what she pointed out to him. She wondered what he still knew. She wondered, if she said the word "Italy" to him, what might come into his mind.

In spite of the obstacles, she flew there a week later and went like an arrow to the heart of Venice where she had reserved a room. They'd missed too much that first time; now that she was here, this seemed so clear. During that last trip, shaken as they'd been by the suicide, exhausted by the heat and the bouncing bus ride into the old city, they'd only spent half a day before moving on. Now she would experience Venice at her leisure; she'd wander the streets alone with her camera and her journal, savoring the oddities and searching for whatever it was that had compelled her to return.

She got up early—she had been getting up at dawn since the day she and Perry stopped sharing the old queen-sized bed— and watched the sky outside her open shutters fill with a brief and intense tangerine light, then settle down for a day of steady, pounding shine. She showered, dressed, and breakfasted on coffee and toast, thinking of her husband spraddled thin and restless on his bed, confused by her absence. What was he dreaming? Did he understand that she would be back?

By the time she emerged on the front steps of the old hotel, the cobblestone streets were hot, and thirsty pigeons were gliding from windowsill to shutter to the waters of the canal. Black cats flashed away in front of her; the smells of floating garbage and urine percolated gently through the simmering, hazy air. She hesitated (Amy was right, I'm *old*, she thought), then pulled her guidebook from her purse. Each narrow, winding street was another passage through the labyrinth, and any wrong turn could lead her off into an abandoned section of the city.

She studied her map for a few moments, then put the book away and began to walk, looking for the arrows that led to Ponte Rialto. Within five minutes she was lost in a maze of haunted streets and wondering if her strength would hold up after all. Why had she come? She still wasn't sure. The city was decaying, and few of the buildings, apparently, had been or were being restored. Rot spread up from the docks and into the houses; plaster fell off in sheets, and everywhere the old bricks were crumbing into dust. Whole buildings were sinking into the canals; doorsteps wavered under inches of water. Everyone was moving out, abandoning history. Everyone was escaping to the industrial centers and harbor towns, where money could be made. Venice was simply too big to save and so it was becoming one vast and crumbling boneyard. Yet, she thought, it was glorious in its decay.

Gargoyles leered down at her; stately Roman busts brooded over heavy doorknockers. She wanted to study the details, but the heat was draining her quickly. Voices drew her along for several more blocks and then she was in an open square: San Rocco. She went up to the doors of the church, thought about going inside, but instead sat down on the warm marble steps to watch a father and his toddler rolling a red ball back and forth beneath a lone, sunshocked olive tree. Pigeons gurgled and pecked among the cobblestones, and a large drab bird, almost hidden among the olive leaves, sang blithely to itself. She leaned back against the wall and half closed her eyes, listening to the father crooning to his child...and then something happened. The thing for which she had come. She recognized that much, though later she couldn't say what, exactly, it had been— only that if she hadn't, at almost seventy, flown like a young girl a quarter of the way around the world to seek it, it never *would* have happened.

Italy—this moment of chipped marble and catpiss and bird-song and the giggling of the black-haired baby—suddenly seemed intensely beautiful, haloed by the other-world glory of her girlhood dream. In her dream, Italy had been a paradise of terraced Tuscan hills and cypress, black against the setting sun. And now she was seeing what she had always known was there but had forgotten for so many years. She held very still, hardly breathing, and felt something ethereal—joy?—brush up against her, purring. Fiery ripples ran up and down the skin of her arms. The light throbbed, the child's laughter was music, she felt herself begin to rise...and in the midst of it she was stabbed by the thought of Perry, a painful sharp longing for him as he had been in the days when she was afraid to love him.

The vision faded slowly and she sat in its pulsing afterglow, thinking about death. For of course he would be gone soon. No matter that he was old and sick—his death would still be ridiculous and inexplicable, but at least she would no longer try to protect herself against it. She'd learned *that* much with Chris. There *was* no defense, no matter what games you thought you were playing with love.

Shana could no longer remember her daughter at fifteen, the way she'd looked at Serenissima walking the lane with her sister. At twenty-eight, however, in the very last stages of metastasized breast cancer, Chris was both horrifying and ethereally beautiful. Shana had been holding ice to her lips; Chris made a pathetic little whimper as though, at the last moment and in spite of the searing pain that had stripped the flesh from her bones, she didn't want to go after all, and then she let out a great sigh and stepped off into air, swinging free. *Good*, Shana whispered fiercely, running the ice over her own streaming eyes. Good for *you*, baby.

For a long moment, sitting there in the strong sun of San Rocco plaza, she was submerged in grief so immediate and severe that it made her shake. Finally she was able to get up and continue on her way, following the arrows toward San Marco and Ponte Rialto. I'm in Italy, she told herself, trying to recapture the transcendent moment. *Italy*...but what came to her instead was the heat, the stink of decay, the faint and ludicrous warbling of a gondolier in some distant canal.

And then she could see Ponte Rialto up ahead, the great arching bridge covered in open shops and fruit stands, and she remembered that other day, how she'd elbowed her way through the crush of tourists and struggled to keep Amy and Chris in view. Her vigilance had not stopped a slick-looking man (not Italian, but some German or Austrian taking advantage of the warm South) from pinching them both, nor had it stopped Perry from lunging after him and almost getting himself punched. She'd pulled him away and held his slight body against hers as he struggled to go after the lecher, who moved casually off into the crowd. They were both panting by the time Perry stopped—and then they were laughing wildly together in light of the absurdity of what they were trying to do: show their daughters the world, yet keep them perfectly safe and untouched. For just a moment she remembered what his body had been like then, the hard and vibrant feel of it against her own—and her moment of shock at how much she loved him, in spite of the years she'd tried to hold him away.

Now she crossed the bridge with the rest of the pilgrims, winding her way through more crowded lanes, until suddenly she came out into an immense square. San Marco. The sun was high and bright over the paving stones. Uniformed waiters guarded empty tables at the cafés lining the square, while beyond them surged the crowds. She stood for a moment looking at the immense sea of moving bodies.

And now the gates to her past opened fully, and the memories flooded over her like the river of people: Perry as a young man, her daughters as infants, her grandmother, middle-aged. The faces she herself had owned—her baby cheeks, her adolescent's eyes, bright with willful courage, her hopeful, trepid wedding-day smile, the mad glare on the face of the corpse in the campground— and she thought of what she might have given up had she given in to the terror, had she taken the rope and climbed up on the chair herself, the way that Perry confessed on that terrible night in Serenissima he feared she would do. Yet he had continued to love her anyway, love her with all his open heart, and when the time came for him to finally leave her, she would live on that.

He'll be in Italy, she thought. The one I dreamed.

All around her people surged in their endless driving activity, camera-and-shopping-bag-laden, dragging their offspring behind them. She stood apart from them, a traveler in their midst, as they pushed through the open doors of the great Byzantine cathedral.

Paula Huston's fiction has appeared in numerous magazines. Her novel, *Daughter of Song*, was published in 1995.

"I'M FREELANCE, THAT'S WHY I'M FASTER."

IN THE ROOM WITH SEVENTEEN WINDOWS / *Kevin Stein*

A surprise child, born in their forties,
had pushed them into this room among the oaks
whose twice-trimmed branches still caressed
the house with a drummer's brushed *shoosh*.
A room so new she'd awaken and stumble
to the walk-in closet to squat on a john
that wasn't beneath her. He'd hear the thump
and her cursing, then reach for the switch
he'd wired too far from their bed.
This time a storm thrashed south of town,
so the sky strobed black to white to black,
as when a child he'd so furiously flicked
the light switch—while his baby-sitter
frugged to *Meet the Beatles*—his pleasure
had worn it out. No click, no light.
Maybe that's what made him want to make love,
something conditioned into him that night,
or something hard-wired all along:
a thought which comforted him as he kissed
her neck and shoulders. She lay still,
eyes focused somewhere above his face.
"What's that sound," she asked,
"something sawing itself in half?"
The katydid, enticing a mate, ratcheted
so passionately their bare walls
reverberated with its frantic cranking.
She couldn't concentrate, imagining
the thing on a branch looking in
one of seventeen windows. Watching.
She made him flip on the deck light,
thinking that would shut it up. Then
a broom to flail low branches and scare it
off: he in boxers and Birkenstocks,
grass wet, the sky light-switching above,
rainwater showering him with each broom swipe.
Still the katydid sang its anthem,

insistent, hopeful, imploring,
a tune which, given his own predicament,
reminded him that daily four people
call Graceland and ask to speak to Elvis.
Seriously. No one needed to tell him
love was the gods' lascivious joke,
so why not—he bent on knee to sing
"Love Me Tender" through the window
screen, just reaching the last plaintive
"...never let me go" as her alarm buzzed
and the katydid, resigned to fate, hushed.

REVENANT / *Kevin Stein*

That March the factory axed me, a neighbor
unclenched my fists with his shovel's consolation.
We planted hardy quince and potentilla,
juniper and the delicate flowering crab.
No, not *we*—I dug their bottomless holes
and grunted each into its appointed place
until his ice-tea-eye winked, *there*.
Bent on knee, I sorted music from static
on the Ford's old Philco, AM crackling
with distant storms, Da Nang's body count,
a slew of acid-induced rock 'n' roll hymns
to the revolution he despised.
We hardly talked—my jaw clamped with
Seventies' anger, his because mine was—
so the joyless task was left to his wife,
flushed-cheeked from peach wine,
to kitchen-corner me with the story
of a boy hidden the day his parents were boxed
to Auschwitz. The false wall, the woman's hand
that brought cold soup, his piss pot
and that single candle. All this,
because he cried amidst blood-red tulips
with black eyes and I'd asked *why*.
The innocent *why* sure to bring on trouble,
the *why* I nailed to the wall this morning
while framing my son's new room.
You know what happens. It's a day like any
other, then a child falls from a fickle oak,
the dog at last surprises a squirrel,
your father calls to say he's misplaced
his good teeth. A day like any other,
the story goes, until the wall you've built
walls off a face lit by candlelight:
a boy on his knees beside the low slot
soup bowls slide through. You close your eyes,
or shutter them with gloved hands,
hoping the vision will flee, and still

it blooms: red tulips with black eyes,
red without. You've seen enough to know
who clutches the soup, whose lips kiss and kiss
the mottled wrist: your neighbor, your son,
never you.

WHAT I HATE ABOUT POSTMODERNISM
/ *Kevin Stein*

As sunrise percolated through spires
of black oak, my son has flung banana slices
on the window, so from *his* angle
the sun's gold face has eyes as off-kilter
as Klee's "Head of a Man"—a model perhaps
of Klee's befuddled father at 6:02 AM,
or Klee thinking of being a father,
one eye focused on joy at hand, the other
on some distant vision of white shoes,
white belt and hat. The End.
Because it's morning the radio's mostly talk,
though the local radio personality slathers
something vaguely obscene over my cold toast.
Six foot six and a mere 142 pounds, he's "Fatman"—
and thus Postmodern. His name, he says, bespeaks
the "irrevocable breach between sign and signified."
He's a gas, as is the fiery thing we signify
by "sun," shedding its first rays on the painting
bought after my glasses snapped and skittered
across polished hardwood: bare lightbulbs
sudden opulent moons, night a thick smudge
spackled with crinolines. I held a lens to one eye,
then the next, like my diabolical Other's monocle,
shifting feet before a three-piece composition
whose every edge aligns so there's no right
way to hang it. No wrong way either,
as my friend explained, in the loft he shares
with a stunning fiction writer. She,
though not his lover, writes each morning
in the nude so he might sketch her breasts
at rest on the formica table top's lip.
Over coffee and onion bagels, at first
they looked a couple, but he was too solicitous
with cream and she with lumps of sugar,
and the newspaper was there only to line
the kitty-litter box, Sunday bra and panty ads

to sketch thin necks, arched thighs.
You think I've gone on, that my lingering over
their marijuana plants propped in wall-high windows
hints of envy—though it's not the fact
but the *idea* of growing pot in windows
which seduces me, that recklessness.
What is envy anyway but the admission
of something absent in your life you hope
to find in the anything of another's,
simple longing devolved into the primary colors
of want blotched across this painting:
the red splotch a cardinal feeding two monstrous
cowbird chicks, their necks raised high
above the bird's scrawny and doomed brood,
his good intentions nothing more than reason
subjugated by pride. And what is pride
but the first sin: an apple of ineffable
loveliness hollowed by bees, and this
a fool's vision. The Beginning.
Be honest: You thought the snapped glasses
were a metaphor. They were just cheap,
a bargaining with gods as redemptive as sun
parting sky to reveal what's already there
though I could not see it,
supple and forgiving at any father's hour.

POEM WRITTEN LATE CENTURY, FULL MOON AT TREELINE, SAN JUAN RANGE, COLORADO
/ *Kevin Stein*

That battered flashlight strung inside
the tent, small sun on a rope, lurches over
wife and daughter and son, then back again,
tracing a shrinking arc across their placid faces.
In the dark, I wonder what life awaits them,
what death? Surely the hour and altitude
make me as ponderous as the emigré poet
whose village burned beneath Nazi parachutes.
The hour and the altitude, or some perversion
of the saying my father's father spoke
at every funeral but his own,
"I'll confess to guilt for my good fortune
if you'll admit to hating me for both,"
spreading grief like jam over peanut butter.
Among stunted pines, a coyote asks, "Who, who?"
and others answer, accusingly, "You, you,"
though death imagined as peanut butter
on white is not the metaphor of an emigré poet,
only lunch at tree line above boulder fields
sprinkled with mine tailings, sulfurous tongues
spilling down ridge where Alfred Packer,
ignoring Chief Ouray's advice, led his party
into the one-way mountains of October.
Snowbound, they died and Alfred ate them,
walked out next June with a sickly grin.
"It's sweet," he said, "like young chicken."
Now restaurants feature *The Packer:*
chicken breast with pickles fingered
around the bun. This, we call marketing.
This explains why I want something to die for.
A revolution. Something larger than the pitiful
cloud my breath makes. I want North Korea
to ban the bomb, Iraq to embrace its Kurds,
Jesse Helms to dance with Carol Moseley Braun.

Really I want to sleep, but the flashlight
pours its small cascade while a spider drops
her skein as if riding the beam's particle and wave,
the sloshing of body against body that accounts
for these sleeping children I want to protect
from the hour and the altitude and spider bite.
Yet *want* is surely the problem, our appetite
as keen as the spider's, all of us
spinning beneath light hung on a rope,
under the dome that thrums with every breath
each of us takes and takes and takes.

Kevin Stein's new book of poems, *Bruised Paradise,* will appear this summer.

WHEN WE WERE WOLVES / *Jon Billman*

A N OREGON BOOT WAS a heavy iron cuff with an iron brace that ran down your ankle and under your arch. The idea of course was to discourage migration. It was invented by some crackpot warden at Salem with too much free time on his hands. We had Oregon boots in Wyoming in 1949, and walking in them was like walking across the exercise yard in ice skates. We did that too.

We learned to act and think as a gang, a team ("There is no 'I' in 'team'!"), apostles. And this is what we saw quickly: Christianity in prison carried privileges. We got what is called "good time," time off our sentences, for attending services. We got free subscriptions to *National Geographic*. We got all the bad coffee we could drink. Instead of making gravel, bucking grain, peeling potatoes or pressing license plates, we dusted pews and crafted nativity scenes out of plywood and wind chimes out of tin fruit-cocktail cans and baling twine.

As Wolves—we were the Wolves—we were well on our way to *really* good time. We wanted to play hockey, and if we had to attend Pastor Liverance's Wednesday Night Bible Study to do it, what the hell, so be it. Like the apostle Paul, we were former Commandment breakers on the road to Damascus. And Cheyenne.

The Hole is where you went for fighting. It didn't matter who started it. We naturally didn't much care for one another, but we learned to suppress our darker instincts for the greater good of the whole. It was teamwork, sportsmanship, brotherly love out of necessity.

"Behold, happy is the man whom God correcteth: Therefore despise not thou the chastening of the Almighty: For He maketh sore, and bindeth up: He woundeth, and His hands make whole," our chaplain told a small congregation of us one early sunny Sunday morning. "Gentlemen: faith and the execution of goodness is your fast ticket out of here."

The Oil Cup was what the best team in the Rocky Mountain Oil League got to keep. The *Purgatory Camera* ran a photo of our governor Brandall Owens hoisting the gold Oil Cup at a flashy press conference in Cheyenne. Pastor Liverance, an ex-Canadian and an ex-hockey player, wanted that cup on his altar in Purgatory like it was the Holy Grail itself. The chaplain sat in on parole hearings and his opinion mattered.

"Gentlemen, I want that cup," he said every afternoon before practice. He said it like a man possessed, a pirate, Captain Crook, staring past us at the sagebrush sea of opportunity that cup would bring for his advancement. We saw it as our opportunity, too. His advancement was our freedom. The Wolves wanted out.

It reads somewhere in Genesis that "While the earth remains, seedtime and harvest, cold and heat, summer and winter, day and night shall not cease," and the Wolves didn't either, in our efforts to master hockey. Most of the time the yard was dry and dusty, and the dirt and sand caked our faces and stuck to our hair oil. When it rained we laced up our skates and practiced in the mud, running up and down the greasy yard in powerful high-kneeing battle stomps, chasing the makeshift puck we carved out of an old snow tire, then slapping it in the general direction of the chicken wire goals. In late October it got cold enough for the wall guards' spit to freeze when it hit the ground, so Warden Gordon had them hose down a quarter-acre section of hardpan that stayed slick and frozen until April (not counting a brief January or February thaw), wherein we skated in the brown slush.

We lifted barbells and dumbbells. We performed sit-ups and jumping jacks. We ran laps in our Oregon boots. We got to where we could skate in a straight enough line without falling down. Our ankles grew strong and knotted. Some days the chaplain would watch the team from the watchtower and yell encouraging words from above. "That's it boys, that's it!" Warden Gordon chose the team color, atomic orange, and our colleagues made our canvas game uniforms in the garment shop.

We got new blue dungarees and striped hickory shirts to wear on the bus. The guys in License Plate honed our blades to razor sharpness. Pastor Liverance passed out brand-new Gideons. We didn't necessarily like each other, weren't buddy-buddy. But we kept our eyes on the pastor and stomped and skated together for a greater good—the good time we would get if Liverance got his Oil Cup.

At night in our dim cells we read stories about Cain and David and Max McNab and Gordie Howe and John the Baptist.

In those days geologists here from Texas and Oklahoma had just discovered oil four miles under the earth in the Cambrian

Layer, and though it was harder to get at than the shallow seas of crude in the South, oil began spouting up all over our high desert. Rookie crude barons with new mad money thought it might be fun to own restaurants and roadhouses and big new Chryslers and Lincolns and hockey teams. They thought it might be even more fun to sell a lot of tickets and pit their hockey teams against a band of hooligans from the Wyoming State Pen.

Governor Owens was a pale, gaunt fellow who saw Wyoming as a colossal gold mine. Brandall Owens thought it sounded like a good idea, therefore Warden Gordon thought it sounded like a great idea. The Wolves took right away to thinking of the whole shitaree as divine.

Pastor Liverance must have thought he was scoring in some big spiritual face-off because he had volunteered out here, was here because he *wanted* to be—the Pope of Wyoming himself. A short man, he teetered around the pulpit on stiff new dogger-heel cowboy boots as he spoke, keeping his arms out for balance as he clunked around the wooden platform, like the tall man on stilts at the rodeo circus or a dude from out East. Or like he was wearing hockey skates in church. He never did get used to those boots and the extra two inches of height with which they endowed him.

"What's your take out here, Pastor?" the Wolves asked at that first Christian rendezvous. No one *wants* to be here. Permanence isn't Western in nature. You take what you can get, or get what you have to take, and move on, get the hell out. *Vamoose.* Looking down and shifting his narrow eyes, he told us: "It says in Luke to sell all that ye have, and give alms. Provide yourselves with purses that do not grow old, with a treasure in the heavens that does not fail, where no thief approaches and no moth destroys. For where your treasure is, there will your heart be also."

"Say, is there a Pope of Wyoming?" I asked one evening during a Bible Study smoke break. "'Cause if there ain't, this guy's trying awful goddamn hard for nothing."

"Yes there is," said Belecki. "Like there's a King of Canada." Rich Belecki was our forward, our ringer and our finisher, though the Wolves rarely started much in the way of offense that he might finish. Belecki was a white-collar, silver-spoon pretty boy previously from British Columbia, who wound up in prison by embezzling money from some oil company slush fund. He'd grown up with the game, and his family sent him valuable things like a radium-dial watch and spanking-new hockey skates. He was forever rubbing down the rich black leather with mink oil. The rest of us had never skated in our lives and some of the figure skates the Salvation Army gave us were *white*. We supposed Liverance would have to settle for martyrdom or governor. Or they could make him warden. He told us we must protect Belecki on the ice at all costs.

On the chaplain's desk in his dank little office behind the chapel was a photograph of Maurice "The Rocket" Richard in his Canadiens uniform, his hair oiled down slick and his arm around Liverance in his white chaplain collar and black wool getup; the pastor's hair was slick and greasy too. Pastor Liverance smiled away like Christmas in the photo—teeth a yellowed gray from the Chesterfields and big fifteen-cent Webster Golden Weddings he was forever smoking—like he was thinking, "This shot will soon look great on my desk." Old Maurice "The Rocket" smiled thinly, like the whole dog and pony show was making him tired. I didn't know who "The Rocket" was until Pastor Liverance showed me his Canadiens scrapbook. Richard was the Candiens' goal-scoring prima donna, and was subjected to many opponents' illegalities on the ice: bad checks.

On the side of the bus we stencilled: WYOMING STATE PENITENTIARY CHRISTIAN WOLVES. I told the team I read in *National Geographic* that packs of wolves brought down camels on this very desert just a few million years ago, and it was those camel bones making the oil men rich today.

Rob LeBlanc, who sounded French Canadian, but who was really a semi-commercial catfisherman and car thief from Cameron Parish, Louisiana, said, "We have oil in the swamps. We have wolves there too and they eat chickens, ducks and rats, and sometimes big things like children."

Jimmy McGhan, an ex-Normandy marine, ex-horse thief and the Wolves' physical leader, said, "Remember, gentlemen, 'a lion from the forest shall slay them' and 'a wolf from the desert shall destroy them.'"

"Yeah," said Fowler, a third-degree batterer and a second-line wing. "And beware of false prophets, who come to you in sheep's clothing but inwardly are ravenous wolves!" The pack of us just looked at each other with foreheads wrinkled.

The license plates on the bus were yellow and said *Wyoming JESUS* in black next to a black cowboy on a black bucking bronco. All away games. All games we lost by digits the scoreboards couldn't handle.

We lost to the Sheridan Savages and the Casper Cutthroats. The Ogden Americans and the Greeley Giants. We got routed by the Vernal Vikings, Rapid City Chiefs, the Fort Collins Grizzlies. Pocatello Roughnecks. Rock Springs Miners, Billings Badgers. And hammered by the Cheyenne Buffalo.

The other teams were manned mostly by Canadian exports: some guys who were maybe on their way up to the NHL, but most who were on their way down from leagues in regions very cold and dark. Men gaining on thirty, even forty, who hadn't learned enough about anything other than hockey in order to make a living. Men who weren't yet willing to give up their game to support themselves as professional cattle thieves or liquor-store robbers. So they found themselves in the Rocky Mountain Oil League, playing in dim and ratty rinks and dodging the beer, the snowballs, the rotten potatoes that were regularly chucked onto the ice by the Oil League fans—who got into more fistfights than the players. But there were worse places to be, which we reminded them when we rolled into town from Purgatory in the Jesus bus.

Our strong suits did not include puck control or shooting. Or skating. We weren't native to it, so we didn't turn or stop much. But we could run. And we could skate as fast and hard as any team in the Oil League. We had conviction and spirit. And Lord! Could we check.

We were the second-hardest checking team in the Rockies, maybe in America, maybe North America. Thirty-five-mile-an-hour, head-on checks. Train wrecks against the boards with a Canadian in between. And the other thing about our checks: we checked as a pack.

McGhan checked the hardest of all of us and he could call the pack with the look on his face—the way his eyes glassed and sparkled under the black bristle of his eyebrows and the gray shine of his furrowed forehead, the way his neck flexed and his nose and jowls wrinkled. He would snarl and light in on a target and

Jon Billman

high-tail it down the ice like a mad monk, and we other Wolves raced and followed McGhan to the kill—"awhooooooooooooooo!" The first Wolf, McGhan, would be all their guy saw—if even him: Whump! Bless you, brother! Then Whump!-Whump!-Whump! And if Lovelock, our goalie, decided to get into this: Whump! That is to say, if the big check was right at the beginning of a period and no Wolves yet paced the penalty box.

Meanwhile the crowd would be screaming and yelling in language not Christian in nature and one of the Canadians—looking over his shoulder, tail between his legs—would have nosed the puck into our goal—and the police sirens wailed and the light behind the net flashed red and the organist played a jazzy Bulgar tune that wasn't at all like a hymn, but which all the fans knew the words to, as greasy vendor items rained down on us and the refs escorted the check victim away on a Big War surplus stretcher. And it would be shoulder slaps and howls on our bench as we changed lines and another five got a shot at them.

But no fighting.

Not with the other teams. Not with each other. Not even if they well deserved a good ear-boxing or a cuff across the gums. No matter that fighting is part of the game, and every other team in the league would be justified in starting what in prison shop talk is called a *riot*. The Governor and Warden Gordon wanted no bad headlines in *Time* magazine, no bad, what they call in politics, *public relations*. They made it clear that a fight would result in the immediate extinction of the Wolves, to hell with any survival instincts we might possess in our genetic makeups.

The other Oil Leaguers didn't know we weren't allowed fisticuffs, and we still intimidated the hell out of them. They figured the first one in the Oil League to mix it up with us would be the first one in the Oil League to cross the Canadian border in a plywood box. They didn't know we weren't that bad. Half of us had never killed anybody. Or that we skated with Jesus, whose game plan didn't include fistfights. But what they didn't know didn't hurt us. So we continued to check like feral dogs, to intimidate the hell out of other teams, to avoid fighting—and to lose games. This in a time when general managers handed players twenty-five bucks under the table for initiating a ruckus. It's what the legions of Oil League cabin fever fans paid to see. It's what the fans wanted to do to each other, would have done if it were *legal*. Sometimes they did it anyway.

Photos of the games appeared in the *Cheyenne Eagle, Rock Springs*

Rocket-Miner, the *Billings Gazette*, under captions like PURGATORY PRISONERS PELTED AGAIN and WOLF ERADICATION UNDER-WAY. Dirty kids knew us by name. Women with animals and flowers tattooed on their skin wrote us letters telling us where their animals and flowers were. We lost on the radio. Live, following Milton Berle's Texaco Star Theater, on the big Cheyenne tower that broadcast us all over the Rockies and deserts surrounding them: 0-21-0.

Then things started to change. Some of the Wolves were slowly picking up the more tame rudiments of the game. It was as though thirty-five-mile-an-hour checks were beginning to bore them. Belecki's adolescent puck control really started to come back to him. Leblanc learned to turn in big arcs to the left and would even abort checks in favor of following the puck. Lovelock the goalie got the hang of staying in the goal crease. Nearly everyone could skate all the way across the ice to the penalty box without falling down. Pastor Liverance became even more inspired and started writing a *book* about Christian prison hockey, a sort of "how to" guide, as he was a real pioneer in the sport. I memorized new Revelations dealing with ice and the end of the world. They let one of our people go. They paroled Lucky Shepard. And early.

One morning we were just boarding the bus for God-knows-where in the crisp winter sunshine and McGhan said, "Wait a minute." The Wolves all looked around and sniffed the air like we knew something wasn't quite right, who-knew-what? and McGhan put his finger on it and said, "Where in heaven's name has Lucky Shepard been? How long we been playing without a backup goalie?" This is when Pastor Liverance told us Lucky had gone home to his mother in Meeteetse two weeks ago. "Think about the game, will ya?" he advised us.

It was like being born again.

We put extra oil in our hair. We did jumping jacks and push-ups twice a day. We had the boys in License Plate hone our blades after every practice and every game. We learned new verses about hope and heaven and committed them to memory, "The Lord looseth the prisoners, let's hit the road!"

"OK, who we playing tonight?" we asked Pastor Liverance, trying to enter the world of the profound. The subject of who we played was beginning to matter to us. For the first time we saw that Christian battle had a direct bearing on our sentences as professional Wolves.

Especially if we were battling the Cheyenne Buffalo.

Cheyenne was different. The Buffalo were owned by a guy named Stumpy Wells, a greasy-rich petroleum tycoon who was forever trying to make up with his billfold for the fact that he was four feet tall. Stumpy always wore a gray eleven-gallon 20-X Stetson (he was bald too) and when he sat on his billfold he was bigger, much bigger than any man in Wyoming. He recruited the best of the worst, guys actually *banned* from Canada, exiled to Wyoming like it was some Egyptian penal colony. Besides being able to really play hockey, these guys were tougher than harness leather. Maybe they'd beat a ref to a bloody carcass north of the border. Maybe they'd killed somebody. Maybe they'd spent time in a Yukon hoosegow, busting rocks on the tundra. We could only guess, which we did. What we did know was that these guys were now Stumpy's toadies, his northern-import goons. They took cheap shots at us—spearing, hooking, boarding, holding, tripping, high-sticking, elbowing, slashing, spitting, punching. And Stumpy's refs got paid by Stumpy to let it go.

Though the Buffalo played in the seedy Bull Barn downtown, Stumpy Wells bought a genuine used blue-smoke-belching Zamboni with working headlights so that their ice was the smoothest and blackest and also the slickest in the Oil League.

And this: The Buffalo had cheerleaders. Stumpy owned a couple of steak houses named Jugs where the waitresses were all very busty and wore lots of bright makeup and tight, pink-fringed cowgirl outfits. The Jugs girls became the Buffalo Gals on their nights off. They tapped out onto the ice in pink cowboy boots between Zamboni swaths and bounced up and down to some Bob Wills 45 that Stumpy picked out himself and played over the fuzzy public address system. There wasn't a Wolf alive who didn't think about what it would be like to begat with one of the Buffalo Gals just once.

They also had a tame buffalo cow, a mangy hoof-and-mouth victim named Petey that a guy in a Wild Bill getup led around the ice between periods. She drank beer and ate corndogs and dropped steaming cow pies on the ice. It was all pretty much a two-bit circus, including the games. The Buffalo checked harder than we did.

The bus ground out of the prison gates and rumbled through downtown Purgatory before turning east onto the highway. "We're on our way to Boomtown, gentlemen," said Pastor Liverance through the sports page of the *Cheyenne Eagle*, and the bus got really quiet except for the buzz of tires on asphalt and the whir of the heater fan blowing out cold air. "Aaaaaahaaaaa," whined Pastor Liverance, imitating Bob Wills in a mousy falsetto, which he did when he was excited—a more frequent phenomenon now that his hockey team had players who could turn. Pastor Liverance's *V* was beginning to stand less and less for *volunteer* and more and more for *victory*. "Gentlemen," he said, waving his pencil like a staff, "I want that Oil Cup on my desk. I want it *next* year. I want to be the spoiler *this* year, tonight."

We still didn't like him. We still didn't much like each other. We still didn't quite trust him the same way we didn't quite trust each other. But we saw that the pastor could help us, and we hated the Buffalo at a primitive level, someplace down deep where we couldn't help what we felt. And as Wolves, we tried our damnedest to love each other the way it says to in John, Peter, Colossians, Thessalonians and Romans. We liked seeing the parole-board-sitting chaplain in high and gracious spirits.

Our pre-game Bible and prayer meeting in the locker room was attended by various wall-eyed members of the sports-page press. Our locker room still smelled like cigarettes—and hot urine since our last limp through town when McGhan pissed on the radiator. The reporters snapped bright photos of us Wolves drinking reconstituted orange drink and chewing 'Nilla Wafers while LeBlanc cited the First Samuel he committed to memory on the bus trip to Cheyenne: "And the behemoth said to David, 'Am I a dog that you come to me with sticks? Come to me and I will give your flesh to the birds of the air and the beasts of the field.'"

"Amen, brother," the pack howled in rough unison to the snap-snap-snap of bright flashbulbs.

"And David said, 'You come to me with a sword and a spear and a javelin, but I come to you in the name of the Lord of hosts, the God of the captives of Purgatory, whom you have defiled.'" The multitudes had come from the jerkwater towns and down from the hills and we could hear the crowd amassing in the smoky arena. They were already booing. "This evening the Lord will deliver you into my hand, and I will strike you down, and cut off your head; and I will give the dead bodies of the host of the Philistines this day to the beasts of the earth; that all the earth may know that there is a God in Wyoming."

The reporters scribbled on their notepads like crazy men. One of them in an expensive Stetson porkpie said, "It mentions Wyoming in First Samuel?" and Lovelock told him, "Well hell, yes."

"Gentlemen, let us pray," Pastor Liverance said. We looked at the reporters from the corners of our eyes until they took the signal and bowed their heads and held their hands together in front of them. "Dear Heavenly Father, for it was you who brought them out of darkness and the shadow of death. You who heareth the poor and despiseth not your prisoners. And though the rebellious dwell in a dry land, you bringeth out those who are bound with chains."

Very somber, as if our old back-up goalie had died and gone to heaven, Lovelock broke the post-prayer silence and said, "Remember Lucky."

"All right, everyone on the ice," Pastor Liverance said.

We skated a couple of laps and, sure enough, were pelted with the Lord's deep-fried bounty as well as cigarettes and other smoking curses from above.

Stumpy stood high in a high V.I.P. box with Governor Owens, in his silverbelly stingy-brim Stetson, and Warden Gordon who drove over in his long gray '50 Lincoln Continental with license plates that read *Wyoming WARDEN*. The three of them smoked twenty-five cent cigars and laughed and elbowed each other, and the Buffalo Gals brought them drinks and lit more cigars with lighters shaped like oil derricks.

The three refs warmed up to an up-tempo organ version of "Three Blind Mice." Cheap bottle rockets and Roman candles popped and fizzled dimly above the dark coliseum ice. We skipped last laps and went straight for the bench to avoid getting peppered in the smoky dimness with an airborne something big and hard. "Ladies and gentlemen," said the announcer, "please note that these athletes skate at speeds of up to fifty miles per hour, and at these speeds a penny from the stands can put an eye out." It began hailing nickels. "Now, please welcome your own Cheyenne Buffalo!" The Buffalo skated by in a yellow and brown streak and rapped the boards in front of our bench with their sticks. The crowd made a pretty impressive stampede sound by stomping on the wooden seats with the leather heels of their boots.

"God bless you, brothers!" we howled as the Buffalo sped past.

The organist played a bouncy barroom tune, and the Cheyenne crowd howitzered more food aimed at our bench. The Buffalo Gals bounced in rare form. Petey dropped another steaming buffalo pie onto the ice. We were wet and sticky with Cokes and beer and mustard. All this before a covey of Cub Scouts ran around the ice with the American and Wyoming Buffalo flags and the dumb bunny behind the organ pumped out the Star Spangled Banner at polka speed.

"Let's play the spoiler tonight, gentlemen," said Pastor Liverance, dodging a corn dog. Meaning of anybody in the Oil League he would like to see not make it into the playoffs because of the Wolves, it was these goons.

And for almost an entire period we *were* spoilers. The spoiler part happened when the puck landed in front of Belecki after the face-off and he shot from mid-ice. It hit their goalie, Guy Somebody's, chest pad, dropped to the ice, and as Guy was about to be checked hard by Leblanc, he panicked and fumbled it with his glove and it fell to the ice again where he kicked it into his own goal with the heel of his own skate and the police light lit up and there was a vast silence in the crowd that turned to awkward boos and hisses. The Wolves scored their first goal ever in their last game against the Cheyenne Buffalo, a feat that would make sports pages across the West and that everyone in Cheyenne would damn well know about. The Wolves were *winning*.

We circled the goal, raised our sticks in the air, and howled at the top of our lungs. This is when the Buffalo began to act like the earwigs in the mess hall when we dropped Tabasco on them.

The Buffalo coach, a guy named Carl Carlsbad, whose nose pressed flat across his face to the left, nearly touching his ear like it was scotch-taped, sent in a hand-picked line of super-enforcers, guys designed to inflict pain and bodily harm. They wanted to hurt us, and they did. We weren't checking—we were *being* checked. We'd gotten a taste of scoring. We liked it. We tried to do it again. We linked passes together. We set up an actual and sincere power play offense that Pastor Liverance picked from a book. We *turned* and *stopped* and the ice sprayed from under our skates like pine whittle chips. We got the wind knocked out of us against the board lettering—EAT AT JUGS, in fat red letters. We took advantage of four of their goons sitting in the penalty box, and we scored again, red lights and all.

And all this without so much as a single rabbit punch—two to zero, Wolves—and yes, it was something while it lasted. And yes, we could almost believe the Lord was skating with us on the frozen field of battle.

It didn't last, though. After two periods of play, the scoreboard high above read like this through the smoke of free cigarettes and blue Zamboni exhaust:

```
BUFFALO        27
WOLFS          02
        EAT AT JUGS
```

But we'd scored two goals. Warden Gordon visited the locker room between periods to call us *his boys* and say, "This will indeed look good on your records." We taped our cuts and faced off and began the last period of our season, hell-bent on scoring again.

We did score again, and that is when they brought out the Big Czech, and our lives as semi-professional hockey players came to a headlong end.

The Buffalo came out at the beginning of the third period performing crowd-pleasing, boredom-induced stunts like honest-to-God double axles. They also came out checking particularly hard, and, while four Buffalo sat in the penalty box, Leblanc snuck the puck into their net, bringing on the lights and howling for the third time in our lives.

We'd caught a rumor the week before of a Cheyenne giant everyone thought was a janitor who spoke rough English in grunts and growls, and who caught mice in the rink with his bare hands and skinned them. And of course a reporter asked him what the hell he was doing and the giant said, "Making a hat." The rumor, apparently, was true. I swear the giant was nine feet tall on skates and five-hundred pounds. He stomped out of the Zamboni gate wearing goalie gear—like a dinosaur or gladiator—but he didn't go to the goal crease.

The Cheyenne crowd went crazy, knowing this would be better than Big Time Wrestling or Texaco Star Theater any day of the week. The organist pounded out a very bad "King Porter Stomp" as the giant in skates skated in awkward, taunting circles, flicking his stick like a blackjack while the Wolves on the bench watched with gums showing. A very fit five-hundred pounds. He left half-inch-deep troughs in the ice where his skates had been.

And he scored goals. This was mainly because we kept well out of his way. We skated around him, watching our backsides, knowing that one mighty swing of that stick would amputate a limb or land us with the Lord or maybe even somewhere else, depending on other systems of judgment outside of Wyoming State Penal.

Lovelock stayed with the net until the very last minute before bailing, but it was shameful what we were letting the Czech do to our pride. Within five minutes of his appearance they scored another ten goals, making the score thirty-seven to three. This was the score when time ran out on Belecki, and he became a martyr.

The Buffalo were parading in circles behind the Czech when the puck squirted out of the herd and Belecki danced it down the ice and into their net for goal number four. The Czech, in awkward pursuit, let out a grunt that raised the hair on the backs of our necks and checked our Canadian Wolf into the boards with a sickening thud that echoed over the crowd. Belecki just lay there, an unconscious pile of pads and blood, helpless in his white-collar näiveté, and something inside all eleven of us—something natural, but from a place deep and dark and forbidden—snapped inside us. Not even waiting for McGhan to call the attack, we fell upon the Czech, a pack of atomic-orange wildness, in what we called in grammar school a "dogpile." My hands and fists felt disconnected, working on their own without conscience, directed from that heart of wildness and boiled instinct all of us possessed.

The other Buffalo circled and watched, not daring to get involved, as we pummeled the giant's body and the ex-chaplain bounced his skull against the ice a hundred, two hundred times, making a slush like cherry snowcone where his head dented the ice and where we spoiled our hopes of this lifetime and very probably the next.

A few months later Wyoming went from a black and greasy state to an orange and atomic promised land. They discovered immense uranium deposits in the Bear Lodge area—Devil's Tower—and the Uranium Boom was on. Former hockey fans lost interest in oil and took to the hills with picnic lunches and Geiger counters, searching for buried treasure.

Brandall Owens lost the next election to a uranium-fat Republican from Casper, but before leaving the governor's mansion he saw to it as promised that the Wolves left hockey for good, and that all twelve of us were buried so far under the penal system that Armageddon was a damn sight more probable in our lifetimes than parole.

The Cheyenne Atomics played bush-league hockey in the South for a year or so before fizzling.

As I near my allotted three-score and ten, I think about the Czech every new day of this life. They say his eight-and-a-half-foot skeleton was displayed in a sideshow that traveled eastern Europe in mule-drawn circus wagons. Though I really don't believe much else, I believe assuredly that when the Wolves fell upon him, he didn't feel a thing. His eyes just glazed over and his soul flew out and went where all ghosts of animals go.

I read in an old yellowed *National Geographic* that there are no more wolves in Palestine. I read in the *Cheyenne Eagle* that there are no more wolves in Yellowstone.

The book, Pastor Liverance's manuscript, is called *Wolves on Ice: Prison Hockey from the Inside Out*. It's long-yellowed, like old teeth, and sits in the corner under a stack of ancient magazines. And every year the parole board refers to it as "a sad history." This morning at breakfast, between stories I've heard a thousand times about Maurice "The Rocket" Richard, Liverance asked me, Say, did I suppose they still had Oregon boots in Oregon? "I doubt it," I told him. In the spirit of progress they have found something else. Our purses have grown old. We are men.

Jon Billman is a wildland firefighter in eastern Washington and western South Dakota. This, along with a forth coming piece in ZYZZYVA, is his first story publication.

St. Burl's Obituary
by Daniel Akst
MacMurray & Beck, 1996, 269 pp.,
$22.95

Burl Bennett, the main character of this food-obsessed comedy
is a three-hundred-pound journal-
ist, restaurant co-owner and would-
be poet and novelist. He makes
his living penning obituaries for the
New York Tribune, and in his spare
time he labors over his latest writing
project, an epic poem about Joseph
Smith, founder of Mormonism. If
he's not writing or indulging his
passion for food, he's shyly court-
ing Norma, a copy-editor at the
paper. Norma likes him and wants
to have sex with him, but asks him
to lose a hundred pounds first—a
goal shared by Burl, who despises
his great weight.

One evening, arriving at his
restaurant, Gardenia's, and antici-
pating a feast of fried squid and
veal saltimbocca, Burl encounters,
instead, the aftermath of a gang-
land killing and comes face to face
with the killer, hit man for a hard-
to-nail Mafia boss. Burl agrees to
testify against the murderer at first;
but after his car explodes and a
stranger identifying himself as "the
Grim Reaper" threatens him, Burl
decides to hide. In a cross-country
flight that is one long banquet (Burl
falls in love with the Midwest's
pies), he heads for Utah, home of
the Mormons and settling place of
Burl's epic subject, Joseph Smith.

Akst's sharp wit and his Ignatius
Reilly-esque protagonist will cap-
tivate readers from the opening
pages—as will the cast of characters he encounters in his picaresque
adventure: Shields, the black detective who is trying to track him down
and bring him back to New York
so he can testify—or is that really
why he's so anxious to find Burl?
Frederic, the renowned chef who
can make a gourmet meal out of
anything Burl brings him; Engel, a
gay half-Tongan, half-German, who
introduces Burl to one of the few
foods he can't stomach: bat; Wanda,
a waitress/cult-member who seduces
Burl because she wants his seed to
help populate her matriarchal cult.

The odyssey of Burl's "death"
and eventual resurrection is classic comedy, full of shifting identi-
ties and offbeat situations, and rude
mocking of death. And on almost
every page Akst regales us with lav-
ish descriptions of Burl's gourmet
meals—which transcend the ordinary, both in the sheer quantity he
consumes, and in the sensual fervor
with which he eats.

Generations of Winter
by Vassily Aksyonov
translated by John Glad and
Christopher Morris
Vintage, 1995, 592 pp., $13

This epic historical novel, originally published in 1994, tells the story of the Gradov family during the Stalin era. The father is a surgeon and an old liberal, the mother part Georgian. The children, like the Karamazov brothers, each take a different fundamental stance toward life. Nina is a poet and a bohemian, Kirill an earnest politico, and Nikita a brilliant military man, married to Veronika, a woman with a weakness for tennis and fine furs.

The first half of the novel takes place during peacetime. It is a rare experience to read such a realistic and compelling account—neither propagandistic nor satirical—of the "better" Stalin years. The reader is entirely caught up in the developing fates of the Gradovs, determined not only by their personalities and by Stalin, but by the underlying chaos of life.

The second half of the book is about World War II, the last in a succession of bitter tragedies to strike the Russians, and the Gradovs in particular.

Generations of Winter has been compared to *Dr. Zhivago* and *War and Peace*. It's an amazing and eminent novel, kept from the rank of those two classics partly by the fact (evident from Aksyonov's many allusions) that the author is acutely aware of writing in their shadows.

Morning in the Burned House
by Margaret Atwood
Houghton Mifflin, 1995, 127 pp., $19.95

Admirers of Atwood's poetry will find her latest collection (the first in ten years) slim, rushed and loose in comparison to her earlier, more substantial works. Atwood writes of the mortality of beauty and the deterioration of the flesh, the quest for love past full-bloom, and the difficulty of terminally ill parents. Sadly, her treatment of these themes is less than moving. In fact the whole fourth section of the book, dealing with the death of Atwood's father, would have been best limited to the final poem, "The Ottawa River by Night," a masterful elegy in which the poet describes her father heading in his canoe " . . . eventually/to the sea. Not the real one, with its sick whales/and oil slicks, but the other sea, where there can still be/safe arrivals."

Still, the collection has its moments. In "A Sad Child," Atwood displays her characteristic skill at describing the grotesque with simple eloquence. "Manet's Olympia" features a favorite Atwood subject: the femme fatale who berates the male voyeur or master who painted her portrait. "Marsh Languages," a clever meta-poem questions the act of poetry and the meaning of language. Some poems take up earlier Atwood projects more explicitly, such as "Half-Hanged Mary," which seems to resonate with Atwood's earlier prose-poem "Reader, I married Him," 'him' being the hangman of a tale from the history of eighteenth-century Quebec, originally published in Atwood's *Two-Headed Poems* of 1978.

In all, *Morning in the Burned House* is an interesting glance into the book of days of a middle-aged woman with a dying father.

Rule of the Bone
by Russell Banks
HarperCollins, 1995, 390 pp., $22

Banks' twelfth novel is the story of a juvenile delinquent named Chappie, who renames himself "Bone" and embarks on what he self-consciously calls "a life of crime" when he pilfers his mother's coin collection to buy marijuana. "Juvenile" is precisely the right adjective to describe Chappie's delinquency. He is callow, sometimes sweet, and he never graduates from crimes of property.

What goes on around him, however, is more hardcore: his biker roommates deal in speed, and a preteen acquaintance is effectively enslaved by a middle-aged pornographer. Halfway through the story, in its only lapse from verisimilitude, Chappie, a white boy, makes his way to Jamaica without a passport. There he ends up living with some major Rastafarian marijuana growers. It is one of the older Rastafari, "I-man," who turns Chappie's life around.

Writing in the first person, Banks does a marvelous job of letting us inside the mind of his young anti-hero. The author mixes punk jargon with teenage views of the cultural geography of upstate New York and of Jamaica, and he sustains the suspense over how far Chappie will fall until the very end of the story. *Rule of the Bone* is Banks' finest novel to date, of nearly the same caliber as another major recent novel about estranged youth, Patrick McCabe's *The Butcher Boy*.

Once Upon a Time: A Floating Opera
by John Barth
Back Bay Books, 1994, 398 pp., $12.95

Part memoir, part daydream, part metafiction, Barth's latest novel is as impossible to categorize as his previous books.

The story begins with Barth and his wife aboard the family sailboat (confusingly named *US*), cruising on the Chesapeake. Enter Tropical Storm Juan, which causes all sorts of problems and becomes a metaphor for the couple's marital difficulties. Just as the storm blows *US* off course, it blows the reader, too, off course and into Barth's funhouse plot. The author/narrator becomes lost in a figurative swamp from his past, as he is forced by his best friend, an amalgam of Jerome Schreiber, white trash punk, and Jerry Scribner, freelance intellectual, to reexamine the high points of his life (some of which are obviously autobiographical and others just as obviously fictitious).

The story becomes a jumble of scavenged memories, directly reflecting the confused state of the intrusive narrator/protagonist. We hear the voices of Barth *the narrator*, Barth *the character*, and one or more Barths of the past. Further confusing things are the metafictional elements of the novel: Barth's writing of the book, one of the novel's many subjects, begins to affect the plot, becoming a sort of self-fulfilling prophecy.

In the end we are unsure whether the subject of the novel was the novel itself or the life of its author. In any case, Barth's prose is, as always, rhythmic, vital and lush; the reader does not so much read *Once Upon a Time* as fall into it.

Painted Desert
by Frederick Barthelme
Viking, 1995, 243 pp., $22.95

Barthelme's sequel to *The Brothers* opens with narrator Del, a forty-seven-year-old junior college professor, and his twenty-seven-year-old girlfriend, Jen, watching the O.J. Simpson car chase on a small TV while riding in a car themselves.

"This is one of those remember-where-you-were-when-it-happened things," Del tells his young lover, who responds: "Duh. Earth to Del. That's not how it works anymore, buddy. Must be a generation deal. So much stuff happens now you couldn't ever remember where you were each time, anyway."

Some things, however, transcend generations, and one of them is Nature, the ace that Barthelme hides up his sleeve for much of this ramble through the total weirdness of the information age, an age which turns up the volume on the most bizarre and sick aspects of humanity. Del is a TV news junkie who watches disasters for aesthetic appeal, and Jen is a "small-scale cybermuckraker." They come off as the models of electronic voyeurism, with a fascination for the most perverse and insane aspects of humanity, which cable TV and the Internet deliver in abundance.

They decide it's time to go to California and, in a phrase that proves how life repeats itself, "get involved" in some intangible way. Thus begins a long, ironic, funny drive west which includes not only Del and Jen, but Jen's father, Mike (only a few years older than Del), and Jen's friend Penny. The two men envy one another's lives for reasons that surprise each of them, and which are discussed at length; but when middle-aged philosophizing and the Kennedy assassination and the other passengers' sensational news fixations threaten to grow old, Jen's intelligence and unpredictability sustain the novel.

Painted Desert occasionally threatens to bog down in its dialogue and contemporary references; and its point about the separate reality created by TV risks being too obvious for prolonged scrutiny. But this turns out to be only part of what Barthelme is after here, and the story's attitude throughout is ironic without belittling its characters. Even at its slowest points, Barthelme saves the moment with his eye for the weird and his surefire wit.

Name Dropping: Tales from My Barbary Coast Saloon
by Barnaby Conrad
HarperCollins West, 1994, 212 pp., $18.00

The forthright title of this memoir lets us kick back and enjoy Barnaby Conrad's stories of the people he met during the 1950s and early '60s, when he owned and ran El Matador, one of San Francisco's hippest bars.

The bar was named for a best-selling novel Conrad wrote in 1952. In addition to giving him the name for his bar, the novel provided him with the connections to attract the best and brightest of the era to his saloon. Tidbits: In the guest book, Charles Addams draws a bull standing proudly above a human's ear; Lenny Bruce mocks flamenco dancers (and anyone else who happens by); Conrad gets Steinbeck a dinner reservation, Steinbeck invites Conrad to the Virgin Islands; Truman Capote mollifies Mrs. Conrad's savage bulldog; Conrad and Bing Crosby go duck hunting; Ingrid Bergman, Marilyn Monroe, Jack Kerouac and Gary Cooper all drop in.

You might expect this to get tiresome after seventy or eighty pages, but Conrad's prose is so smooth (if banal from time to time) and his attitude so self-effacing, you don't get bored. In other words, Conrad is an awfully good name-dropper. The book is lively, funny and frivolous, a delightful confection.

Asian-Pacific Folktales and Legends

Edited by Jeanette Faurot
Touchstone, 1995, 252 pp., $12.00

I picked up *Asian-Pacific Folktales and Legends* hoping that I might be able to find in it some of the old Vietnamese fables my mother used to tell me but which she could never remember in enough detail to satisfy me. Initially I was disappointed that of the sixty-one stories, only six were identified as Vietnamese.

As I began to read them, however, I realized that while each story is ascribed to a certain country, the assignment is not very strict. Many of the countries represented in Faurot's anthology are close together culturally as well as geographically; thus a story identified in the book as Chinese may be one that is traditionally told in some of the other countries as well.

The stories, which come from China, Korea, Japan, Indonesia, the Philippines, Malaysia, Thailand and Vietnam, are grouped into five sections according to structure and type. They range from simple fables to exquisite and complex tales. Many are creation myths or explanations of natural phenomena; others address the beliefs and history of the particular culture in which they originated.

Faurot has wisely avoided taking artistic license with the stories; the accuracy of this anthology is one of its greatest strengths. A sort of Asian-Pacific version of Edith Hamilton's *Mythology*, it's been a long time coming for the academic set. It's also a book I'll let my mother read.

Harriet Beecher Stowe: A Life

by Joan D. Hedrick
Oxford, 1994, 507pp., $15.95

Harriet Beecher Stowe became the pre-eminent female literary voice in nineteenth-century America and author of the most influential American novel of the nineteenth century, despite being mired in what she called the "tide mud" of domestic duty. She fought not only the limitations imposed on her gender, but the male literary establishment, some of whom automatically dismissed anything written by a woman as "sentimental" or "didactic."

With a cultural historian's attention to detail, biographer Joan Hedrick parts the curtain on nineteenth-century New England, where Stowe was born in 1811, as well as on the frontier town of Cincinnati, where she lived from 1832 to 1850. She depicts family life—prevailing birth control practices and the general attitude toward children. She also describes the early, revolutionary education of women, the use of alternative medical procedures and the development of American literature alongside the emergence of the parlor literary club and the publishing industry. In addition, she details the evolution of such epochal movements as women's suffrage and abolition.

Not until we are near the midpoint of this book do we see Stowe as more than a bit player: daughter of Lyman Beecher, New England cleric and patriarch; sister and apprentice of Catharine Beecher, pioneering educator; wife of the Bible scholar, Calvin Stowe. At this point Hedrick begins to rely extensively on Stowe's letters to friends, family and business associates to bring her subject to center stage.

Hedrick gives a careful account of Stowe's long and influential writing career. Stowe was both a writer and a mother, who hired a girl to do the household chores and a nurse to care for the children so she could write for three hours each day. She was clear about one thing: she did it for the money. As the wife of a poorly paid seminarian, she was under pressure to be principal breadwinner for her expanding family.

Stowe produced seventeen books, as well as many newspaper and magazine articles, and she made a good living at it. But she struggled in her early years against poverty and frequent pregnancies, and later against bereavement as four of her seven children died. Ultimately her reputation as a writer suffered also, when what Hedrick calls "the masculinization of literature" took over American letters.

Practical Magic
by Alice Hoffman
G.P. Putnam's Sons, 1995, 244 pp., $22.95

The eleventh novel from the doyenne of "Yankee Magical Realism" is as compulsively readable as it is slightly embarrassing to like.

Gillian and Sally Owens, orphaned sisters, have been raised by their two maiden aunts, whose weirdness—they are viewed as witches by the people of the small New England town where they live—leaves the girls yearning for normalcy. Sally is the practical sister who keeps the household running. Black-haired Gillian is the wild one who stays out all night. Yet both girls have the same response to the love-crazed women who come to their aunts for spells and potions to solve their romantic problems: "Yuck!" The two vow never to be ruled by their passions.

On the subject of passions, Hoffman waxes eloquent, if hyperbolic.

The girls learn from firsthand observation that "a woman could want a man so much she might vomit in the kitchen sink or cry so fiercely that blood would form in the corners of her eyes." Unfortunately, Hoffman relies too much on such extravagant descriptions to embellish what is basically a sound, if not riveting story.

Sally and Gillian grow up and not surprisingly, they go different ways. Sally marries, has two daughters and is eventually widowed; Gillian runs through a string of no-good men, culminating in the supremely no-good Jimmy, a man so nasty that "on the day they moved into their rented house in Tucson, the mice had all fled because even the field mice had more sense than she did." Jimmy is an out-and-out sleaze; he peddles drugs to kids and abuses Gillian, who, contrary to her long-ago vow, adores him. His untimely end is what reunites the two sisters, provides the conflict for the remaining three-quarters of the novel, and eventually forces Sally and Gillian to embrace their ancestry as spell-weaving, potion-brewing Owens women.

If you can put up with the redundancy and clichés (all the women in this book are heart-breakingly beautiful, all the men are magnetic, and adult love is always signalled by the characters wanting to "fuck all night,") you'll find yourself getting caught up in the story. Hoffman knows how to keep a narrative moving and when she's not overwriting, her prose is excellent; she also has a true gift for evoking mood.

If this novel lacks the depth and moral weight of the best fiction, it nevertheless entertains in an accomplished, graceful style.

Virginia Woolf
by James King
W.W. Norton, 1994, 699 pp., $35

One wonders, upon reading of Woolf's frustrations with writing the biography of friend and Bloomsbury compatriot Roger Fry, what she would have thought about this massive effort to re-create her own life in these nearly 700 pages, exhaustively documented with selections from her letters, essays, reviews and books. "I work my brain into a screw over Roger—what did he do in 1904—when did his wife go mad, and how on earth does one explain madness and love in sober prose, with dates attached?" wrote Woolf. "The artist's imagination at its most intense fires out what is perishable in fact... but the biographer must accept the perishable, build with it, imbed it in the very fabric of his work."

Given the biographer's difficult task of working with the "perishable," King does a creditable job when he sticks with his professed purpose: to "look closely at how [Woolf's] novels and other writings reflect the search for the distinctly feminine aesthetic, one in which the intuitive parts of the self are dominant." But any biographer of Woolf would be tempted to dwell in the slightly scandalous corners of her life, and unfortunately King succumbs to temptation. Using ambiguous or evasive snippets from Woolf's letters and journals, he speculates about the psychosexual underpinnings of her relationships. Whenever he seems perplexed about the complexity of Woolf's sexual identity he quickly points to half-brother George Duckworth's molestation of the young Virginia as the basis for her adult sexuality.

The strongest sections of the biography are those that fulfill King's stated purpose, explicating Woolf's writing, and describing her attempt to illustrate "the flight of the mind." Her writings revealed her conception of the artist as someone who tried to "attain a different kind of beauty, achieve a symmetry by means of infinite discords... some kind of whole made of shivering fragments."

Students, and even casual readers of Woolf, will find wading through King's biography valuable. If King's psychoanalysis of his subject is superficial, his textual criticism is solid; and in the generously quoted raw material of the book, Woolf's voice emerges, strong and vital—and clearly not perishable.

Tom: The Unknown Tennessee Williams
by Lyle Leverich
Crown, 1995, 626 pp., $35.00

Leverich's fascinating new biography of Tennessee Williams covers Williams' life until *The Glass Menagerie* opened in early 1945. The play, Williams' first incontrovertible success (he was in his mid-thirties), is about a family's frustrated inability to express and receive love and their retreat into separate dream worlds. Its mood of hapless, crazed aloneness reflected his own family experience and would remain one of his lifelong subjects.

In 1932, Tom Williams (he later concocted the nom de plume "Tennessee" for a literary contest) was in his third year at the University of Missouri, flunking out of ROTC for the third time. His father, Cornelius, finally said enough is enough, took him out of the university and installed him in a $65-a-week job as a stocker in the shoe company where he was a sales manager. Tom lived at home in St. Louis for three years, drinking coffee all night, writing, going to work in the daytime at the factory. His father paid his medical bills and was responsible for his employment, yet the two of them never communicated except negatively, and Williams would sneak out the back door rather than face his father. Meanwhile, Tom's sister, Rose, was slipping from eccentricity into schizophrenia. Tom somehow managed to continue writing, to audit writing classes at Washington University, and to keep sending stories and poems out to little magazines despite hundreds of rejections.

The combination of pain, mental volatility, frustrated caring, and brave effort in this slice of Williams' life was typical of his early years. His mother, Edwina, never gave up her fantasy world of Southern gentility or her fierce protectiveness of her son. Accustomed to being taken care of by his mother, Williams might not have made it through the thicket of his early career if he hadn't found a mother-figure/literary agent in the person of Audrey Wood. Wood responded to Williams' lost and vulnerable quality. He wrote her marvelous, indulgent, self-revealing (but sometimes partly fictionalized) letters about his latest misadventures.

Leverich makes no bones about the fact that Williams was more enjoyable on paper than in the flesh: He had a shrieking, hysterical laugh and was inconsiderate and unkempt to the point of grossness; he bummed money and never paid it back, was socially awkward and generally disliked conversation. Yet despite his social impairments, Williams maintained several long-term friends and supporters among those with a keen appreciation for literature, artistic integrity, and hard work. He was an indefatigable worker, constantly spitting out rewrites of his short stories and plays.

Leverich's biography is a chronological account that does not challenge the known basic outline of Williams' melodramatic life. It is not a "concept" biography but an honest digging in the diaries, letters, and memories of Williams and the people who knew him. It is a marvelous read for those interested in Tennessee Williams and also for those who are curious about the milieus of the twenties through the forties, from St. Louis and New Orleans to both coasts.

Grassland: The History, Biology, Politics and Promise of the American Prairie
by Richard Manning
Viking, 1995, 306 pp., $23.95

Unlike recent celebrations of the American grassland—Ian Frazier's *Great Plains* and William Least Heat Moon's *PrairyErth* come to mind—*Grassland* is a lament. Manning traces the history of human destruction of the plains, from early extinctions caused by Neolithic hunters, to the virtual elimination of the bison in three years, to the less dramatic but equally devastating introduction of European mono-culture farming, irrigation and exotic grasses late in the nineteenth century.

European settlers of the plains were convinced that Nebraska could look like Pennsylvania. They laid down a grid made up of 160-acre sections, applying the pastoral Jeffersonian ideal to land that received (and still receives) less than ten inches of rain per year. These yeomen plowed up the prairie and eventually got, in return, the dust bowl.

From the 1930s to the early 1970s, the federal government went to extraordinary lengths to ensure that the plains never again turned to dust. Farmers were encouraged to maintain substantial hedgerows and practice fallow-strip farming and crop rotation. But Earl Butz, Nixon's Agriculture Secretary, reversed this advice, urging farmers to plow from "fencerow to fencerow" and to focus their efforts (and machinery budgets) on only one crop. American agriculture hasn't looked back since, and in the last sixty years we've never been closer to the conditions that led to the dust bowl.

The environmental devastation of the plains is a problem, Manning argues, not just because nature is pretty, but because erosion and loss of plant diversity—which go hand in hand—endanger the sustainability of land that is capable of producing huge amounts of food virtually forever.

Grassland moves from the history of the plains to present-day problems to solutions, but Manning often gets sidetracked, dwelling on grassland minutia (the histories of each of a dozen-odd native grasses, for example). Despite his efforts to stay firmly grounded in reality, Manning's proposals for restoring the plains sometimes seem far-fetched. He posits that eating buffalo or grass-fed cattle is environmentally preferable to vegetarianism (which depends on mono-culture farming and irrigation) and proposes that we turn much of our cultivated land over to grass and grazing. In Richard Manning's future, Americans would sit down at tables brimming with the products of the native plains. Here Manning's vision begins to

break down, for while it is not impossible to imagine the U.S. as a nation of buffalo eaters, imagining us relishing rolls made from the crushed seeds of multi-cropped native grasses requires some suspension of disbelief. While *Grassland* conveys a palpable sense of the "promise" of the plains, it doesn't, finally, propose a feasible means of regaining that promise.

The History and Power of Writing
by Henri-Jean Martin
Translated by Lydia G. Cochrane
Chicago, 1995, 591 pp., $18.95

This spectacular survey of the history of writing causes us to wonder, among many other things, about the continuing tradeoffs that are made as one era transforms into another. The Bible was composed during a thousand-year period by people who believed in the magical power of the word, the ability of certain utterances to create or destroy or manipulate cosmic forces. By the time Plato was writing in the fourth century B.C., however, he had at his disposal a flexible and widely enough used written language to question and even scorn the religions of past oral cultures with their shape-shifting, immoral gods. The ability of writing to isolate and define abstract concepts helped secularize law and philosophy. Yet in *Phaedrus*, Plato reports Socrates' opinion that the invention of writing (by Theuth, an Egyptian god) would destroy people's memories.

Oral culture was hardly done for, however. The system of jurisprudence practiced in Rome was based on oral deliberations and dialogue. Roman authors like Cicero composed orally, memorized their compositions, then dictated them to scribes—which is why Roman writing can be wordy, repetitious, and contradictory. Reading was done aloud or with lip movement well beyond the first thousand years A.D.

From the tenth through the thirteenth centuries, scholastic thinkers believed in the power of logic with the same degree of naiveté as ancient peoples believed in the power of individual utterances, charms, and spells. Every part of St. Thomas' *Summa theologica* is laid out in careful, rational order; to demonstrate something by means of logic was to make it so. Grammar was regarded during the Scholastic Age as the superior language discipline due to the latent assumption that there was a correspondence between the laws of thought and language.

The increasing power of writing depended on technological innovations, including the inventions of papyrus, the preferred writing medium for Romans, and later of parchment. Unlike papyrus, parchment could be produced all over Europe and it was so sturdy that parchment books were sometimes bleached and used a second or third time. However, parchment had a serious disadvantage: it cost a herd of sheep to produce a bible. Paper, made of a slurry of rags and fiber (hemp being commonly used), was a good compromise in terms of price and durability. The widespread use of paper and the fully established use of cursive script made possible an explosion of writing, and consequently of access to writing, in the thirteenth and fourteenth centuries. Until that time, writing and books were so rare that books were chained to desks in the Sorbonne and so valuable that a theology stu-

dent who owned three books was considered well-off.

Henri-Jean Martin points out that at every transition in the history of writing something is lost and something gained. With the spread of writing and literacy in the fourteenth century, semieducated clerics and laity could begin to know and to question—making way for the beginnings of the Reformation and the Age of Humanism. The losses included the loss of the sense of the power of language of ancient peoples, and the decreased abililty to compose, comprehend, and memorize without aid of books of the Classic Age.

This is an elegant book, comprehensive yet full of precise, interesting detail. We give it our highest recommendation.

In the Cut
by Susanna Moore
Knopf, 1995, 180 pp., $21

In Moore's three previous novels the protagonists were pretty, girlish young women stranded between their Hawaiian origins and life in the big city (New York or Los Angeles). Here the nameless protagonist is at home in New York City—enough at home to go to clubs late at night, and to know where the best places are for catching a cab. She is enough of a New Yorker, too, to embark on a thrilling and dangerous erotic adventure.

The heroine is a single English professor. One of her ill-educated students, Cornelius, under the guise of needing help with his homework, begins to trail her. One evening, during an ambiguous meeting in a bar with Cornelius, she goes in search of a bathroom and accidentally witnesses a redheaded stranger engaged in a sex act. The heroine turns out to be the last person to see the redhead alive. The detectives assigned to the murder keep turning up wherever the narrator goes, ostensibly to question her. She nonetheless refuses to cringe or to give up her freedom of movement. In fact, she begins a heated affair with one of the detectives.

The suspense is unremitting. We keep thinking, "This woman shouldn't be doing this," but what she's doing is exciting (Moore has a real gift for writing dirty) and should be permissible in an ideal, feminist world.

The narrator is interested in linguistics—she is compiling a dictionary of street slang—and Susanna Moore has an amazing ear for the speech of the Irish detective, Malloy, and the poor black kid, Cornelius. Yet there is something about the narrator's always listening to the words rather than the emotion that heightens our uneasiness.

In the Cut is several excellent novels in one: an old-fashioned *roman noir*, a cautionary tale for feminists and a study in the hazards of taking people literally. It is one of the best novels of 1995.

World Fire: The Culture of Fire on Earth
by Stephen J. Pyne
Henry Holt and Company, 1995, 384 pp., $30

In this definitive work, fire-geographer Stephen Pyne tells us that he intends "to bring to a larger audience something of the significance of fire on Earth." His mission is as worthy as any of the numerous environmental causes that have won popular support in recent years. After years of persuasion by conservationists and environmentalists, we now know that wolves are a vital part of the natural order, not simply adventure-story villains whose only function is to bankrupt sheep ranches. Likewise, while most of us view fire as an aberrant phenomenon, some people are beginning to realize that as the ancient Greeks taught, fire is elemental, and no more alien to our planet than water and wind. Pyne shows us that the forest fires that terrify us in the news are not isolated, but part of one flame that is consuming the world on the installment plan, preparing the ground for new growth. For Pyne, the problem is not fire prevention. It is fire-consciousness and control.

Pyne wants us to realize that we humans are "fire creatures." The first really effective thing we did to make our environment hospitable was to set fire to it. Humans have set fires to stabilize ecological systems, such as grasslands, from the beginning of time.

To support his thesis, Pyne mixes one part poetry with one part science. *World Fire* moves freely from ornate and erudite catalogs of literary and historical references to charts and scientific analysis. Sections of the book, with dexterous cultural references to fire, previously appeared in magazines as disparate as *Antaeus* and *Natural History*. Part philosophical treatise and part textbook, it is an indispensable anatomy of fire.

New Stories from the South: The Year's Best 1995
Edited by Shannon Ravenel
Algonquin Books of Chapel Hill, 1995, 265 pp., $10.95 (paper)

"It's about the end of things," says Thomas Laswell, a recent college graduate in Caroline A. Langston's story "In the Distance." He is speaking of his favorite movie, *Last Tango in Paris*, but his pronouncement could just as well be used to describe the seventeen stories in the most recent *New Stories from the South*. The stories in this tenth anthology capture pivotal moments that mark the ends of old lives and the beginnings of new ones. And they catch us up in this change by vividly depicting the characters as they struggle to understand exactly how their troubles began.

Susan Perabo's "Gravity" is the story of Alex and Jessica, two sixth-graders who accidentally kill the class bully during a hike in the woods. Alex, tortured by guilt, wants to turn herself in, while Jessica, calloused by the experience, does not. What is certain is that their friendship dies with their indecision. In "Riding with Doctor," by R. Sebastian Bennett, a pretentious folklorist, referred to only as "Doctor," is abducted by the female members of the Cajun folk group he is studying. The women view their inventive torture of him as a fitting end to their relationship with a man who has condescended to them once too often. The narrator in Wendy Brenner's "I Am the Bear" feels a momentary sense of power when she dresses up as a polar bear for a grocery store promotion. And when she is kissed by a teenage model who assumes she is a man, the narrator knows what it is to be in control. Yet her feelings of supremacy are short-lived, once she learns that she must keep on being the bear to maintain her power. Finally, "Drummer Down" by Barry Hannah lets us reflect with Paul Smith on his relationship with an older student, Drum, and on Drum's recent suicide. Though Paul would like to idealize the man whom he remembers "foggily as a god"

involved in the "war against evil," the poem that Drum leaves behind makes the death of his romantic notion inevitable.

The voices in these stories—old, young, black, white, male, female, rich and poor—are as varied as the stories themselves; yet, what finally unites the stories are the characters' yearnings to survive the inevitable endings that they face.

Zod Wallop
by William Browning Spencer
St. Martin's, 1995, 278 pp., $21.95

Harry Gainesborough is a children's author whose talent dries up when his young daughter, Amy, drowns. Following her death he checks into a psychiatric hospital, and as part of his therapy begins to write a new book, *Zod Wallop*.

Unlike his previous books this one, influenced by his grief, is a horrifying children's fairy-tale-gone-bad, in which all the heroes die and there is no happy ending. When Harry leaves the hospital, one of his fellow patients embarks on a mission to bring the book to life, drafting hospital patients to play the roles of Gainesborough's characters. Harry is drawn into the delusion, and soon the strange cast finds itself being followed by two sinister rival pharmaceutical companies vying for their capture.

When parallels to *Zod Wallop* begin to occur in real life, Harry realizes that his invention is more than just another story. As events progress, the boundaries between fact and fantasy break down and Harry finds himself faced with a difficult moral dilemma.

Spencer's narrative dexterity and the astute social commentary in his children's book-within-a-book make this more than just another fantasy novel.

The Hundred Secret Senses
by Amy Tan
G.P. Putnam's, 1995, 358 pp., $24.95

Amy Tan's latest novel recreates the experiences of women trying to reconcile the differences between Chinese traditions and American rules of conduct. Tan's previous best-selling novels, *The Joy Luck Club* and *The Kitchen God's Wife*, were laden with mystery and magic from Chinese lore. Like those two books, *The Hundred Secret Senses* is an intricate, colorful tale that revolves around family.

It is the story of Asian-American Olivia, who through her relationship with her half-sister, Kwan, attempts to find love in her loveless marriage to Simon. Olivia first meets Kwan after the death of their father, when Kwan comes to live with Olivia, her two brothers and her neglectful American mother. Kwan quickly becomes Olivia's surrogate mother, and entertains and frightens her younger half-sibling with her tales of ghosts and ancestors, and the superstitions of ancient China. Olivia gets the opportunity to reexamine Kwan's secret stories when her marriage to Simon begins to deteriorate, and Kwan takes them on a trip over the bridge of reason into the land beyond, the mystical and foreign depths of China.

Tan's superb prose, her vivid depiction of Chinese tradition and her ability to plumb the depths of sisterhood, love and family make this a fascinating read.

Kyrie
by Ellen Bryan Voigt
W.W. Norton, 1995, 80 pp., $17.95

Between March 1918 and March 1919, Spanish influenza killed more than twenty-five million people worldwide, including half a million in the United States alone. The Western world was at war, but the flu epidemic took more lives than all the modern killing machinery of that war combined.

Ellen Bryan Voigt's new collection of terrifying and celebratory sonnets imaginatively recreates voices lost in the pandemic: a soldier writing home, his schoolteacher fiancée, a traveling doctor, a traveling preacher, the orphaned children, widows and widowers.

In a series of poems that begins with the dark specter of an eclipse and closes in a stripped and barren field of winter wheat, Voigt's vivid characters put a human face on this massive loss. Their individual testimonies climb and blend into a single human voice singing against the plague: "Sweet are the songs of wry exacted praise,/scraped from the grave . . . to the god who thought to keep us here"

Reviews by:
Virginia Fick, Reeves Hamilton, Kristen Harmon, Willoughby Johnson, Diedre Kindsfather, Mike Land, Speer Morgan, Hoa Ngo, Sarah Oster, Kirsten Rogers, David Schlansker, Jim Steck, Evelyn Somers, Kris Somerville, Sam Stowers, Jeff Thomson, Melissa Wright

THE
PUSHCART
PRIZE
XX

1996

BEST
OF THE
SMALL
PRESSES

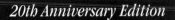

20th Anniversary Edition

Edited by
Bill Henderson
with the
Pushcart Prize
editors

This book is essential.
■ LIBRARY JOURNAL

Those who despair of finding good writing in mass media America need look no further than the Pushcart Prize.
■ BOOKLIST

Of inestimable value... as intelligent an introduction and thoroughly enjoyable a sampling as one can find.
■ VILLAGE VOICE

Striking in its literary breadth and accomplishment.... There is so much to choose from here that readers may not want to choose at all — they can just read on and on and on.
■ PUBLISHERS WEEKLY (starred review)

The single best measure of the state of affairs in American literature today.
■ NEW YORK TIMES BOOK REVIEW

The range and amount of good writing in this volume defy anyone's attempts at representation and summary.
■ WORLD LITERATURE TODAY

An invaluable guide.
■ LA READER

JUST PUBLISHED
570 PAGES
CLOTH BOUND **$29.50**
PAPERBACK **$16.00**

PUSHCART PRESS • P.O. BOX 380 • WAINSCOTT, N.Y. 11975